**The Author**

A professional caterer since 1968, Jo-ann
Schoenfeld is known throughout New York's
Westchester County for the imaginative dishes
she creates for major social events. At her
home in Hastings-on-Hudson, she conducts
a popular two-month class (there's always a
waiting list) specializing in cake decorating
and party menus.

Jo-ann Schoenfeld

# THE READY AIM COOKBOOK

Hopkinson and Blake, Publishers, New York

Copyright © 1976 by Jo-ann Schoenfeld

Published by Hopkinson and Blake
185 Madison Avenue, New York, N.Y. 10016

Manufactured in the United States of America
by Noble Offset Printers, Inc., New York

---

**Library of Congress Cataloging in Publication Data**

Schoenfeld, Jo-ann, 1932-
    The ready aim cookbook.

    Includes index.
  1.  Cookery.  2.  Stuffed foods (Cookery)
3.  Kitchen utensils.  I.  Title.
TX652.S36       641.5'86      76-54151
ISBN 0-911974-27-X

printing number

            8   9   10

# Contents

*Cover photo: Gâteau Saint-Honoré*

## Hot Hors d'oeuvres

## Main Courses and Accompaniments

# Introduction

The Ready Aim Cookbook was especially designed for the electric foodgun, and it is intended to help you use this appliance to the best advantage.

One of the main features of the foodgun is its ability to achieve exciting visual effects —to make food more appealing to the eye. The recipes in this book were fashioned to serve that purpose.

In short, the aim of this book is to guide you in preparing dishes that taste delicious *and look terrific.*

If you've longed for the opportunity to show your creativeness with food, you have it now. If your family and friends are only too familiar with your repertoire, here's the chance to spring some surprises.

This collection combines classic recipes that have been adapted for the foodgun, some standard recipes that have been augmented for special decorative effects, and many new ones that the enterprising cook will find rewarding. All the recipes have been tested by a panel of home economists.

The range of recipes is broad enough to accommodate every need . . . snacks for the children, family dinners, canapés for casual guests, and gala dishes for important festive occasions. Some are quite elaborate, and the cook who seeks an interesting challenge will find these especially inviting. Others are simple, and although they require only a little of your time, they will guide you in producing dishes that reflect true culinary artistry. Whether fancy or simple, or some-where in between, the recipes offer a host of ideas for using conventional ingredients (and some exotic ingredients as well) in new and imaginative ways.

If you find joy in creating beautiful dishes, great adventures lie ahead.

# Cooking with the Electric Foodgun

The electric foodgun is a new kitchen appliance designed to help you prepare deliciously decorative foods quickly and easily.

## It's a Canapé Glamorizer

The foodgun is perfect for creating professional-looking canapés. You can load it with cheese spreads, meat or fish mixtures, or pâtés and turn out attractive snacks in seconds. You can prepare appetizers right on your serving plates just seconds before your guests arrive, so canapés never get soggy. Or you can freeze them in advance and pop them into the oven at a moment's notice.

## It's a Stuffer

Filling pasta, cream puffs, eggs, vegetables and tartlette shells is a breeze. The foodgun does the work. You just squeeze the trigger.

## It's a Decorator

With the foodgun, you can transform a simple cake into a thing of beauty in seconds. You can use the gun to dress up an otherwise ordinary main dish with a whipped potato crown. Or you can pipe icing swirls or frosting flowers on a pastry base to achieve a truly dazzling dessert.

## It's a Cookie and Candy Maker

Nine design discs plus a decorator tip make shaping attractive and uniform cookies a snap. And you'll find it easy to sandwich cookies together with frosting or to decorate them in just about any way that suits your fancy. The foodgun is also ideal for shaping mints and other candies.

## It's an Idea Creator

When you've learned the basic tricks of the trigger, you'll find dozens of new ways to express your creativity.

## SUGGESTIONS FOR DECORATING

To master the techniques of decorating, it's a good idea to practice. Fill the foodgun with softened cream cheese or ricotta cheese. Using cookie sheets and round baking pans, practice making kisses, stars, swirled rosettes and decorative borders. With a little experience and experimentation you'll soon be creating your own designs.

### Using the Decorator Tip

For kisses, stars and swirled rosettes the foodgun should be held upright with the tip lightly touching the surface being decorated.

*Kisses (mounds):* Hold in position and squeeze the trigger. When mixture begins to mound, raise the tip with it, but keep the tip slightly buried. Then release the trigger and move away.

*Stars:* Hold in position and squeeze the trigger just long enough for the star to form; then move away.

*Swirled rosettes:* Hold in position and squeeze the trigger. When mixture begins to mound, raise the tip with it, moving up and away with a circular motion.

*Borders, lattice toppings, pastry straws and cookie fingers:* The foodgun should be held at a 45-degree angle to the surface being decorated or to the cookie sheet. Raise the decorator tip slightly above the surface. Always work toward yourself. Squeeze the trigger continuously. As soon as the mixture begins to flow through the tip, move the foodgun toward yourself, making sure that the tip is slightly above the surface.

### Making Pressed Cookies or Fudge

Line up several cookie sheets. Fit the foodgun with the disc specified in the recipe. Stand the foodgun upright on the cookie sheet, with the barrel cap firmly touching the sheet. Squeeze the trigger continuously, and as each cookie or fudge form is released, move on to the next spot.

### Some General Comments

It's best to apply decorations as close to serving time as possible. The foods will appear fresher and there will be less chance of having your delicate decorations bruised.

Don't overlook the finishing touches. When decorating desserts you can achieve a professional touch by sprinkling grated chocolate, grated nuts, or grated cake crumbs on the finished product. When decorating salad molds or hors d'oeuvres you might want to add another bit of color or texture with a sprinkle of freshly chopped parsley, nuts, or slices of fruits or vegetables. In planning your menu expand your thoughts beyond the selection of foods that complement each other. Think about color, texture, shape.

### Your Kitchen Is Your Studio

In a very real sense, the preparation of beautiful foods is a medium of artistic expression. You have all the elements at hand—color, texture and shape—with which to sculpt an expression of your own artistic instincts. You can be as inventive, as original, as your own sense of design will allow. Break away from the mundane. Be creative. Your kitchen is your studio.

**Using the Foodgun:** As you get accustomed to the foodgun, you'll make the necessary adjustments automatically. Be sure the dough is not too hard or too soft. Ingredients must be finely ground or chopped to avoid stringing or blocking of discs or tips.

| The Situation | The Explanation | The Easy Adjustment |
|---|---|---|
| Dough doesn't release from disc. | Dough is too hard. | Remove cap and disc; run dough through foodgun at high speed; allow to stand at room temperature until softened. |
| Dough comes through disc onto baking pan but is sticky and doesn't shape well. | Dough is too soft. | Refrigerate until dough is firmer. |
| When decorator tip is used, mixture strings out instead of mounding or swirling. | Decorator tip is raised too high above surface. | Keep decorator tip buried slightly in mixture as it comes through tip onto surface. |
| Dough doesn't work well with particular disc. | Choice of disc. | Use only discs specified in recipes. |
| Dough breaks when using decorator tip to make lattice topping, cookie fingers or pastry straws. | Foodgun is being pulled too rapidly toward you. Tip is lifted too high above surface. | Move foodgun a little more slowly. Hold it at a 45-degree angle to surface. Keep decorator tip slightly above surface. |
| Mixture doesn't come through decorator or filler tip. | Ingredients are too coarse. | *Nuts:* grate in blender and strain. *Chocolate:* grate in blender. *Vegetables:* chop very fine or press through fine blade of meat grinder. *Meats:* press through fine blade of meat grinder or whirl in electric blender. |
| Refrigerated hors d'oeuvre fillings won't go through decorator tip. | Mixture is too hard. | Bring to room temperature and soften with wooden spoon. |
| Mixture continues to flow from decorator tip after trigger has been released. | Pressure inside barrel. | Release trigger shortly before you want flow to stop. |

## INCIDENTALLY...

### Butter

Although butter is called for in many of these recipes, it's all right to substitute margarine. Since butter and margarine will give equally good results, follow your taste — or pocketbook — preference.

### Onions

Many of the recipes call for grated onion rather than minced or finely chopped onion. If you would rather chop or mince, remember that the onions must be fine enough to flow through the foodgun.

### Spinach

Cooked spinach must be very well drained before it is used in the electric foodgun. Place it in a strainer and press out all the water with the back of a wooden spoon.

### Meat grinder

When a recipe instructs you to use a meat grinder, the aim is to process ingredients so they will flow through the foodgun easily. If you don't have a meat grinder, chop the foods until they are fine enough to be pressed through the foodgun. Do not use an electric blender unless a recipe specifically calls for it, because the resulting consistency may be undesirable.

### Leftover bread

There's no need to waste bread that's left over from a recipe. To make bread crumbs, arrange bread pieces in a single layer on a baking sheet. Bake in a preheated 350-degree oven for 10 to 15 minutes until the bread is dry and toasty. When the bread is cool, break it into smaller pieces and whirl them in an electric blender until fine. Store the crumbs in a jar with a tight lid.

### Herbs

Fresh herbs have an aroma and flavor that can't be matched. Cooks who have used fresh garlic, dill, chives and parsley— which are available in most areas—almost always prefer them to the dried variety. However, when fresh herbs are unobtainable, dried herbs will serve. As a general rule, ¼ teaspoon of dried herbs equals 1 teaspoon of fresh herbs.

### Whipping cream

To whip heavy cream, pour it into a large bowl set in a bigger bowl filled with ice water. This will help keep the cream cold and thus speed up the whipping process. Use a wire balloon whisk, a hand electric beater, or a rotary beater—whichever is most comfortable for you. If you are adding sugar or flavorings, do so when the cream begins to mound softly. Cream sweetened with confectioners' sugar and whipped over ice water is less likely to turn into butter and will not separate when left standing.

### Beating egg whites

Always bring egg whites to room temperature before beating them. However, it's easier to separate eggs when they're cold, so do this when you first take them out of the refrigerator. The bowl and the beaters must be dry and clean. Place the whites in a large bowl and beat them, using either a wire balloon whisk or an electric beater, until they are stiff but not dry.

### Eggs

When you're left with unused egg yolks or whites, try storing them in a plastic ice cube tray. Place one yolk or white in each cube section and freeze. Once they're frozen, pop them into a plastic bag and seal it well. Then you can use the individual yolks or whites as needed.

**Scallions**

In some parts of the country scallions are known as green onions. Don't be misled by the different terms; the food is one and the same. In these recipes, they are called scallions.

## EQUIVALENT MEASURES

| | |
|---|---|
| 1 tablespoon | 3 teaspoons |
| ¼ cup | 4 tablespoons |
| ⅓ cup | 5⅓ tablespoons |
| ½ cup | 8 tablespoons |
| 1 cup | 16 tablespoons |

## EQUIVALENT AMOUNTS

| | | |
|---|---|---|
| Broth | 1 bouillon cube or 1 envelope powdered broth base dissolved in 1 cup boiling water | 1 cup |
| Butter | ¼ pound stick | ½ cup |
| Cheese | ¼ pound | 1 cup grated |
| Coconut, flaked | 3½-ounce can | 1⅓ cups |
| Cream, heavy | ½ pint (1 cup) | 2 cups whipped |
| Gelatin, unflavored | 1 envelope | 1 tablespoon |
| Lemon | 1 medium | 3 tablespoons juice 1 tablespoon grated rind |
| Nuts, shelled | | |
| Almonds | 1 pound | 3 cups |
| Peanuts | 1 pound | 4 cups |
| Pecans | 1 pound | 4 cups |
| Walnuts | 1 pound | 4 cups |
| Onion | 1 medium | ¾ to 1 cup chopped |
| Orange | 1 medium | ⅓ to ½ cup juice 2 tablespoons grated rind |
| Potatoes | 1 pound | 3 medium |

## GUIDELINES FOR REFRIGERATING

**Hors d'oeuvres on breads:** Line the bottom of a baking pan or plastic container with damp (not wet) paper towels to prevent the breads from drying. The pan or container should be deeper than the hors d'oeuvres to protect the decorations. Place the hors d'oeuvres on the damp paper. Cover tightly with plastic wrap or aluminum foil. Bakery boxes can also be used but must be lined first with aluminum foil, then with damp paper towels.

**Fillings:** Store in containers with tight lids or in bowls sealed with plastic wrap or aluminum foil.

**Molds:** Store in the mold pans, tightly covered with plastic wrap or aluminum foil. Unmold and decorate on day of serving.

## GUIDELINES FOR FREEZING

**Hors d'oeuvres:** Freeze in a single layer on cookie sheets. When frozen, place carefully in plastic bags, tie tightly, and immediately replace in freezer. To heat, place *frozen* hors d'oeuvres on cookie sheets.

**Fillings and sauces:** Store in several *small* well-capped containers. This way you can defrost as much or as little as you need.

**Decorated desserts:** To avoid bruising the decorations, place *unwrapped* dessert in freezer. When frozen, place in plastic bag or wrap securely in aluminum foil and store in freezer.

**Defrosting desserts:** It's best to defrost frozen desserts in the refrigerator (still covered).

**Reheating frozen foods:** Allow at least the original baking time. Foods already defrosted require a shorter reheating period.

# Cold Hors d'oeuvres

# Cold Hors d'oeuvres

You don't need exotic ingredients to create exotic appetizers. Everyday staples — like spinach, cheese, tuna — are the inexpensive, ready-at-hand bases for dozens of distinctive fingerfoods. With a little imagination — and a flick of the trigger — you can create platters of beautiful, tantalizing tidbits. What's more, you'll have as much fun making them as you will eating them.

**Preparing Ahead:** The cold canapé spreads can be prepared a day or two in advance and refrigerated. Then, just before serving, you can pipe them on to crackers and breads. Trims, garnishes and other embellishments should be added at the last moment. Your foodgun enables you to apply these impressive finishing touches in a twinkling!

## Whole Wheat Cones

Delicious when stuffed with Roquefort Gardens mixture, Simple Salmon Chive Pâté or other cold fillings.

*Diet-thin whole wheat bread (30 slices per pound)*
*Melted butter*

**1**   Using a 2½-inch round biscuit cutter, cut out one bread round from each slice of bread. (Leftover bread can be made into bread crumbs and saved for other recipes.)

**2**   Shape into cones, pressing overlapping edges together firmly with fingers.

**3**   Place on ungreased baking sheet. Brush inside and outside of cones lightly with melted butter.

**4**   Bake in preheated 350-degree oven for 7 to 10 minutes until lightly toasted. Remove from pan; cool on wire rack.

**5**   Fill with cold hors d'oeuvre mixture, using decorator tip.

Makes about 30 cones.

---

*Variation:* Whole wheat cones may be used untoasted, but should be fresh.

## Coconut Stuffed Apricot Canapés

The apricots make an unusual base for a canapé and are an exciting taste change. Try stuffing them with other fillings as well.

¼   *cup walnuts*
⅓   *cup flaked coconut*
  4   *ounces cream cheese*
2½   *dozen dried apricot halves*

**1**   Grate nuts until fine in blender or Mouli grater. Then place in strainer and sift into bowl. Reserve nut pieces remaining in strainer for garnish.

**2**   Add coconut and cheese to bowl; mix thoroughly.

**3**   Lay out apricot halves, open side up.

**4**   Fill gun with cheese mixture. Fit with decorator tip.

**5**   Using gun at low speed, pipe single swirls of mixture into apricot halves. Do not mound high or the apricots will be overwhelmed. Sprinkle with reserved nut pieces. Refrigerate.

**6**   Serve at room temperature.

Makes 2½ dozen canapés.

## Strawberry Kisses

Delectable and dietetic—under 10 calories each.

*Large fresh strawberries, washed, dried and hulled.*

*Ricotta cheese*

*Ground nutmeg (optional)*

**1**   Cut each strawberry in half. Lay strawberries out, cut side up.

**2**   Fill gun with cheese. Fit with decorator tip.

**3**   Using gun at low speed, pipe ricotta kisses on each strawberry half. Sprinkle nutmeg over ricotta, if desired. Refrigerate.

## Curried Date-Nut Log

A suggestion of sweetness plus a tantalizing tang . . . what a provocative blend of flavors.

  8  *ounces cream cheese*

  1  *cup pitted, chopped dates*

½  *cup chopped walnuts*

½  *to  1  teaspoon curry powder*
    *Toasted coconut*
    *Curried Cream Cheese Garnish
      (recipe follows)*

**1**   In a bowl combine cheese, dates, nuts and curry powder (begin with ½ teaspoon, taste after blending; add more if needed). Mix well. Refrigerate for 1 hour until firm.

**2**   Shape cheese mixture into a log 5 or 6 inches long. Roll in toasted coconut. Pat gently to imbed coconut.

**3**   Fill gun with Curried Cream Cheese Garnish. Fit with decorator tip.

**4**   Using gun at high speed, pipe two or three decorative lines along the length of the log. Refrigerate.

**5**   Serve with crackers and breads for spreading.

Makes 3 dozen hors d'oeuvres.

### Curried Cream Cheese Garnish

  3  *ounces cream cheese, softened*

½  *teaspoon curry powder*

Thoroughly combine cheese and curry powder. Chill if necessary before using in gun.

## Kissed Date
## and Nut Squares

Serve as a sweet hors d'oeuvre . . . or a post-dinner petit four.

½ cup butter, melted
1 cup granulated sugar
2 large eggs, well beaten
¾ cup all-purpose flour
¼ teaspoon baking powder
1 cup chopped walnuts
1 cup chopped dates
8 ounces cream cheese, softened

**1**  With a wooden spoon, mix melted butter with sugar. Add eggs, flour, baking powder, nuts and dates; beat well.

**2**  Spoon mixture into a greased 9x9-inch baking pan. Distribute evenly. Bake in preheated 350-degree oven for 25 minutes or until wooden pick inserted in center comes out clean.

**3**  Remove pan to wire rack; cool for 20 minutes.

**4**  Cut cake into small squares; remove from pan. Cool to room temperature.

**5**  Fill gun with cream cheese. Fit with decorator tip.

**6**  Using gun at high speed, pipe a kiss on each square. Refrigerate.

**7**  Serve at room temperature.

Makes 3 dozen squares.

## Stuffed Gouda
## or Edam Cheese

Change a bland cheese into a grand cheese. All it takes is a little wine, a little butter, a little cheese . . . and a little imagination.

1 2-pound Gouda or Edam cheese (at room temperature)
3 tablespoons dry white wine
1 tablespoon Dijon mustard
¾ cup butter (at room temperature)
¼ cup heavy cream
Salt (optional)

**1**  Slice off top of cheese. Scoop out all cheese from top section; discard shell. Scoop out cheese from bottom section, leaving shell about ½ inch thick. Reserve bottom shell.

**2**  Mash all the scooped cheese with a fork. Place in mixer bowl with wine and mustard. Beat at medium to high speed until creamy.

**3**  Add butter and heavy cream; beat well. Taste for seasoning; add salt if needed. Refrigerate for 1 hour.

**4**  Fill gun with cheese mixture. Fit with decorator tip.

**5**  Using gun at high speed, pipe mixture into the cheese shell, swirling decoratively. Refrigerate.

**6**  Serve at room temperature with crackers for spreading.

Makes about 6 dozen hors d'oeuvres.

## Cucumber Mold

Diced cucumbers in a suave sour cream setting. Very appetizing. And you can serve it as a salad, too.

2   tablespoons butter

¼   cup chopped onions

2   cups unpeeled, diced cucumber
      (1 large cucumber)

½   cup finely diced raw potato
      (1 medium potato)

1   cup chicken broth

2   sprigs parsley

1   teaspoon salt

¼   teaspoon freshly ground black pepper

¼   teaspoon dry mustard

1⅓   envelopes unflavored gelatin

⅓   cup cold water

1½   cups sour cream

1   unpeeled medium-size cucumber,
      seeded and finely diced

      Paprika

**1**   Melt butter in saucepan. Add onions; sauté until soft. Add 2 cups cucumber, potato, broth, parsley, salt, pepper and mustard. Bring to a boil and simmer for 15 minutes until potatoes are tender. Remove from heat.

**2**   Sprinkle gelatin over cold water to soften. Add to cucumber mixture; stir to dissolve. Remove to electric blender and purée. Chill.

**3**   When just about to set, add 1 cup of the sour cream and the diced, seeded cucumber. Mix well.

**4**   Spoon into 1-quart mold; refrigerate until firm. Unmold on serving platter.

**5**   Fill gun with remaining ½ cup of sour cream. Fit with decorator tip.

**6**   Using gun at low speed, pipe decorative border around bottom of mold. Swirl a large rosette on top. Sprinkle lightly with paprika. Refrigerate.

**7**   Serve with crackers and breads for spreading.

Makes 5 dozen hors d'oeuvres.

# Mushroom Mousse

Delicious as a prelude . . . equally delightful as a side dish.

¼  *cup butter*

1½  *cups finely chopped onions*

1½  *pounds mushrooms, sliced (reserve 5 or 6 large mushroom caps, unsliced)*

1½  *tablespoons lemon juice*

1½  *envelopes unflavored gelatin*

⅓  *cup cold water*

2  *tablespoons sherry*

2  *teaspoons salt*

2  *cups sour cream*

1  *clove garlic, pressed*

¼  *cup heavy cream*

**1**  Melt butter in 2-quart saucepan. Add onions; sauté until tender. Add sliced mushrooms and lemon juice. Cook over medium low heat for about 5 minutes, stirring once or twice, until mushrooms are cooked through and have rendered their juices. Remove from heat.

**2**  Sprinkle gelatin over cold water to soften. Add to hot mushroom mixture; stir well to dissolve. Cool completely.

**3**  Add sherry, salt, sour cream and garlic; stir thoroughly. Spoon mixture into a 5- to 6-cup fancy ring mold. Refrigerate until firm.

**4**  Unmold mushroom mousse onto serving platter. Arrange reserved mushroom caps on top of mousse, stem ends down.

**5**  Whip heavy cream until stiff.

**6**  Fill gun with whipped cream. Fit with decorator tip.

**7**  Using gun at low speed, pipe rosettes on top of mushroom caps. Refrigerate.

**8**  Serve with crackers or breads for spreading.

Makes 6 dozen hors d'oeuvres or 12 side-dish servings.

## Roquefort Gardens

You can smell the flowers!

4 ounces Roquefort or blue cheese, softened
4 ounces cream cheese, softened
½ teaspoon Worcestershire sauce
8 pitted Spanish black olives
6 slices firm rye or pumpernickel bread
Softened butter

**1** Press Roquefort cheese through strainer into bowl. Add cream cheese and Worcestershire sauce; mix thoroughly. Refrigerate for 2 hours.

**2** Fill gun with cheese mixture. Fit with star disc.

**3** Using gun at high speed, press out cheese flowers onto baking pan, following instructions for making pressed cookies (see page 9). Refrigerate in pan until firm.

**4** Slice olives into 24 rounds, about ¼-inch thick.

**5** Cut out 4 bread rounds from each slice of bread using a 1½-inch biscuit cutter. Spread a little softened butter on each bread round. Remove cheese flowers from pan with spatula. Place 1 flower on each bread round. Press olive rounds into the centers of the flowers. Refrigerate.

**6** Remove from refrigerator ½ hour before serving.

Makes 18 to 24 canapés.

## Egg Anchovy Mountains

2-ounce can rolled anchovies with capers, drained
5 slices firm white bread
Softened butter
4 medium hard-cooked eggs, sliced
4 ounces cream cheese
2 drops green food coloring

**1** Slice each anchovy roll in half, making 2 full circles.

**2** Cut out 4 bread rounds from each slice of bread using 1½-inch biscuit cutter.

**3** Spread a little softened butter on each bread round. Cover with an egg slice; top with anchovy circle.

**4** Combine cream cheese and coloring; blend well.

**5** Fill gun with cheese. Fit with decorator tip.

**6** Using gun at high speed, pipe a decorative peak on top of each anchovy. This will be easy to do if you hold the anchovy between the thumb and forefinger of one hand while piping cheese with the other hand. Refrigerate.

Makes 20 canapés.

## Spinach and Egg Dome

Inexpensive and delectable!

  8  *large hard-cooked eggs, shelled*
 ¾  *cup finely chopped onions*
 ½  *cup finely chopped scallions*
  2  *cups washed, well dried finely chopped raw spinach*
1½  *teaspoons salt*
  6  *tablespoons mayonnaise*
     *Egg Garnish (recipe follows)*

**1**  Place eggs in a large bowl; mash finely with a potato masher.

**2**  Add onions, scallions, spinach, salt and mayonnaise. Mix well. Taste; add more salt if needed.

**3**  Press mixture into a 1-quart bowl. Refrigerate for at least 2 hours.

**4**  Turn out onto serving platter.

**5**  Fill gun with Egg Garnish. Fit with decorator tip.

**6**  Using gun at high speed, pipe a continuous, up and down U-shaped design around bottom of dome.

**7**  Serve with crackers and breads for spreading.

Makes 3 to 4 dozen hors d'oeuvres.

### Egg Garnish

 2  *large hard-cooked eggs, shelled*
 2  *tablespoons butter*
 1  *tablespoon mayonnaise*
 ½  *teaspoon mustard*
 ⅛  *teaspoon salt*

**1**  With a wooden spoon, press eggs through a fine strainer into a bowl.

**2**  Add other ingredients; mix well. Chill before using in gun.

## Smoked Salmon Fingers

These canapés are truly finger-licking good!

1½  tablespoons butter
 ½  cup very finely chopped onions
 ⅓  pound smoked salmon, very finely diced
  8  ounces cream cheese
1½  teaspoons snipped dill or ¼ teaspoon dried dill weed
 11  firm, thin squares of pumpernickel

**1**   Melt butter in fry pan. Add onions; cook over low heat until soft. Cool.

**2**   Place smoked salmon and cream cheese in a bowl. Using a wooden spoon, mix thoroughly until cheese looks pink.

**3**   Add dill and cooled onions; mix well.

**4**   Remove crusts from bread. Cut each slice into 4 equal finger lengths.

**5**   Fill gun with salmon mixture. Fit with decorator tip.

**6**   Using gun at high speed, pipe mixture onto each bread finger, covering the length of the bread. Refrigerate.

**7**   Serve at room temperature.

Makes 44 canapés.

## Simple Salmon Chive Pâté

8-ounce can salmon, drained (remove bits of bone, skin, etc.)
 4  tablespoons butter, softened
 2  tablespoons finely snipped chives
 ½  teaspoon horseradish
    Salt and pepper to taste
 1  or 2 medium-size cucumbers

**1**   In a bowl, flake salmon with fingers very well, until there are no chunks. Add butter, chives, horseradish, salt and pepper; mix thoroughly. Refrigerate for about 1½ hours.

**2**   Slice cucumber into rounds ¼-inch thick.

**3**   Fill gun with salmon pâté. Fit with decorator tip.

**4**   Using gun at high speed, pipe decorative salmon mounds onto cucumber slices. Refrigerate.

Makes 18 to 24 canapés.

———

*Variation:* The pâté can also be piped into Whole Wheat Cones (see recipe, page 17). When serving it this way, it's best to fill cones at the last minute.

# Smoked Salmon Mousse

An elegant blending of fish, cheese and sour cream . . . cool and refreshing.

1 envelope unflavored gelatin

¼ cup cold water

⅓ pound smoked salmon, diced into
⅓ inch pieces

8 ounces cream cheese

1 tablespoon horseradish

1 tablespoon grated onion

2 tablespoons snipped dill

2 cups sour cream

Smoked Salmon Mousse Garnish
(recipe follows)

1   Sprinkle gelatin over cold water to soften. Stir over hot water to dissolve. Set aside to cool.

2   With mixer at medium to high speed, beat salmon with cheese. Add horseradish, onion, dill and sour cream. Mix thoroughly with a spoon.

3   Add cooled gelatin; mix well. Spoon into a 4-cup mold. Refrigerate until firm.

4   Unmold on serving platter.

5   Fill gun with Smoked Salmon Mousse Garnish. Fit with decorator tip.

6   Using gun at low speed, pipe rosettes around bottom of mousse. Make a large swirl on top, in the center.

7   Serve with crackers, rye and pumpernickel breads for spreading.

Makes about 4 dozen hors d'oeuvres.

## Smoked Salmon Mousse Garnish

¼ cup heavy cream

1 teaspoon snipped dill

1 teaspoon horseradish

Whip heavy cream until thickened. Add dill and horseradish; whip until stiff.

# Cold Dilled
# Salmon Soufflé

1½ envelopes unflavored gelatin

⅓ cup cold water

¾ cup hot chicken broth

¾ cup mayonnaise

1½ tablespoons lemon juice

2 tablespoons grated onion

1 tablespoon snipped dill

1½ teaspoons salt

1 teaspoon Tabasco sauce

1-pound can salmon, drained (remove bits of bone, skin, etc.)

1½ cups heavy cream

3 ounces cream cheese

1 tablespoon sour cream

7 tiny sprigs of dill

**1** Prepare a 1-quart soufflé dish with a paper collar (see directions, page 111).

**2** Sprinkle gelatin over cold water to soften. Add hot broth; stir to dissolve gelatin. Set aside to cool.

**3** Add mayonnaise, lemon juice, onion, dill, salt and Tabasco to cooled broth. Chill until it just begins to set.

**4** With fingers, flake salmon very well until there are no chunks. Add salmon to gelatin mixture; stir well.

**5** Whip heavy cream until stiff. Fold into salmon mixture.

**6** Fill prepared soufflé dish with salmon mixture; smooth top gently with a rubber spatula, making it flat and even. Refrigerate for several hours. Remove collar.

**7** Blend cheese and sour cream.

**8** Fill gun with cheese mixture. Fit with decorator tip.

**9** Using gun at high speed, pipe 6 rosettes around outer edge of soufflé and 1 rosette in center. Place a tiny sprig of dill on each.

Makes over 100 hors d'oeuvres when spread on crackers; 10 to 12 appetizer servings; or 8 luncheon servings.

# Curried Tuna Chiffon

If you're not a curry fancier, this will make you a convert.

2 envelopes unflavored gelatin
⅓ cup cold water
2 cups hot chicken broth
¾ cup chopped onions
¾ cup chopped celery
2 tablespoons butter
2 tablespoons curry powder
2 7-ounce cans tuna fish, drained
¼ cup chopped parsley
½ cup finely chopped walnuts
1 tablespoon lemon juice
1 teaspoon salt
1 cup mayonnaise
Walnut halves
Curried Cream Cheese Posies
(recipe follows)

1 Sprinkle gelatin over cold water to soften. Add to hot broth; stir to dissolve. Set aside to cool completely.

2 Sauté onions and celery in butter for 10 minutes, until tender. Add curry powder; stir. Remove from heat.

3 Place tuna in a large bowl. With fingers, flake very well until there are no chunks. Combine with parsley, chopped walnuts, lemon juice, salt and mayonnaise.

4 Add onion mixture; stir thoroughly. Add completely cooled broth; stir.

5 Pour into 5-cup ring mold. Refrigerate until firm.

6 Unmold onto serving platter. Make circle of walnut halves on top of ring. Place Curried Cream Cheese Posies between walnuts. Refrigerate.

Makes 6 dozen hors d'oeuvres when spread on crackers or breads; 10 to 12 appetizer servings; or 8 luncheon servings.

## Curried Cream Cheese Posies

4 ounces cream cheese, softened
½ teaspoon curry powder

1 Combine cheese and curry powder; mix thoroughly. Chill if necessary before using in gun.

2 Fill gun with curried cream cheese. Fit with star disc.

3 Use gun at high speed. Press out star flowers onto waxed paper-lined baking pan, following directions for making pressed cookies (see page 9). Refrigerate.

4 When flowers are firm, remove from paper. Use as decorations.

## Shrimp Pâté

2 12-ounce packages frozen shelled, deveined shrimp, cooked
5 tablespoons butter, softened
½ teaspoon salt
1½ tablespoons horseradish
⅓ cup mayonnaise
1 clove garlic, pressed
6 tiny sprigs of parsley

**1** Set aside 6 shrimp of same size in refrigerator. Press balance of shrimp through fine blade of a meat grinder into bowl.

**2** Add butter and mix well. Add salt, horseradish, mayonnaise and garlic; blend thoroughly. Reserve ½ cup of the mixture for garnish.

**3** Place balance of the pâté in a small round serving dish. (A 3-cup soufflé dish would be fine.) Press mixture down with rubber spatula, smoothing the top surface until absolutely flat.

**4** Fill gun with reserved pâté mixture. Fit with decorator tip.

**5** Using gun at high speed, pipe 6 swirls around the outer edge of the pâté. Place reserved shrimp between each swirl, facing in the same direction. Stand a sprig of parsley in each pâté swirl.

**6** Serve with crackers and breads for spreading.

Makes 3 to 4 dozen hors d'oeuvres.

---

*Variation:* Shrimp pâté may be piped directly onto bread rounds, cucumber slices or Whole Wheat Cones (see recipe, page 17).

## Crab and Water Chestnut Canapés

2 6-ounce packages frozen crabmeat, thawed and drained (remove all bits of shell, cartilage, etc.)
2 tablespoons butter, softened
2 tablespoons mayonnaise
2 tablespoons lemon juice
2 tablespoons grated onion
2 teaspoons sherry
  Salt and pepper to taste
8-ounce can water chestnuts, drained

**1** Press crabmeat through fine blade of a meat grinder into a bowl. Add butter; mix thoroughly. Add mayonnaise, lemon juice, onion, sherry, salt and pepper. Blend well. Taste for seasonings.

**2** Slice water chestnuts in half horizontally, making two flat rounds from each.

**3** Fill gun with crab mixture. Fit with decorator tip.

**4** Using gun at high speed, pipe small mounds onto each water chestnut half. Refrigerate.

Makes about 3 dozen canapés.

## Herbed Creamed Scallops

When these ravishing rounds of scallop make the rounds they'll be the talk of the table.

*Cooked Sea Scallops (recipe follows)*
*8 ounces cream cheese*
*2 cloves garlic, pressed*
*2 tablespoons finely snipped dill*
*2 tablespoons finely chopped parsley*
*2 tablespoons mayonnaise*

**1**   Cook scallops as directed. Slice cold cooked scallops in half, forming 2 rounds from each.

**2**   Combine other ingredients in a bowl; mix thoroughly.

**3**   Fill gun with cheese mixture. Fit with decorator tip.

**4**   Using gun at high speed, pipe mounds of cheese onto scallop halves. Refrigerate.

Makes about 4 dozen canapés.

### Cooked Sea Scallops

*½   cup dry white wine*
*½   cup water*
*½   teaspoon dried thyme*
*½   bay leaf*
*1   small onion*
*    Sprig of parsley*
*2   peppercorns*
*1   pound sea scallops (as even in size as possible)*

**1**   Simmer wine, water, thyme, bay leaf, onion, parsley and peppercorns in a saucepan for 5 minutes.

**2**   Add scallops and enough additional water to just cover ingredients. Bring quickly to a simmer. Cover pan; continue simmering for exactly 4 minutes.

**3**   Using a slotted spoon, quickly remove scallops from pan. Cool.

## Ham and Cheese Julienne

6  *thin, firm slices white or rye bread*
   *Softened butter*
¼  *pound sliced boiled ham*
¼  *pound Swiss cheese*
   *Mustard Butter Topping*
     *(recipe follows)*

**1**  Remove bread crusts. Spread butter on bread; cut slices into quarters.

**2**  Cut ham into very thin strips, the same length as the bread quarters. Cut cheese the same way.

**3**  Place several ham strips on one half of a bread square, and several cheese strips on the other half. Arrange each bread square this way.

**4**  Fill gun with Mustard Butter Topping. Fit with decorator tip.

**5**  Using gun at low speed, pipe a rosette in center of each bread square, half on ham and half on cheese. Refrigerate.

**6**  Serve at room temperature.

Makes 2 dozen canapés.


### Mustard Butter Topping

¼  *cup butter, softened*
1  *tablespoon prepared mustard*
Thoroughly mix mustard and butter.

## Chicken Nutwiches

Everybody loves a nutwich. These are especially fetching.

1  *cup cooked chicken pieces*
½  *cup mayonnaise*
1  *tablespoon finely snipped chives*
¼  *teaspoon salt*
   *Pepper to taste*
6-ounce package of pecan halves

**1**  Press chicken through fine blade of meat grinder into bowl. Add mayonnaise, chives, salt and pepper; blend well.

**2**  Lay half the pecans out, flat side up. Spread ¼ to ½ teaspoon of chicken mixture on each pecan. Top with reserved pecan halves to form sandwiches. Turn sandwiches up so they are sitting on a long seam.

**3**  Fill gun with balance of chicken mixture. Fit with decorator tip.

**4**  Using gun at high speed, cover top seam of each sandwich with a single decorative piping. Refrigerate.

Makes 4 to 5 dozen canapés.

*Shown right, Egg Anchovy Mountains (p. 22), Ham and Cheese Julienne (p. 30), Strawberry Kisses (p. 18), Smoked Salmon Fingers (p. 24), Coconut Stuffed Apricot Canapés (p. 17), Roquefort Gardens (p. 22).*

## Ricotta Spinach Poulet

Great for weight-watchers. About 18 calories per tablespoon.

  2  *cups cooked chicken*
 ¼  *cup cooked spinach, well drained*
2½  *cups ricotta cheese*
  2  *tablespoons grated onion*
  3  *tablespoons lemon juice*
     *Salt and pepper*
     *Cherry tomatoes (optional)*

**1**   Press chicken and spinach through fine blade of a meat grinder into a bowl.

**2**   Add two cups of cheese, onion and lemon juice to chicken mixture. Mix thoroughly. Taste; add salt and pepper as needed.

**3**   Place on serving platter; shape into a rectangular loaf. If too soft to shape, refrigerate until firm; then shape.

**4**   Fill gun with remaining ½ cup cheese. Fit with decorator tip.

**5**   Using gun at low speed, pipe decorative border around top of mold. Place cherry tomatoes on platter around mold.

**6**   Serve with crackers for spreading.

Makes about 6 dozen hors d'oeuvres.

———

*Variation:* Fill gun with chicken mixture. Fit with decorator tip. Pipe into raw mushroom caps or cherry tomatoes, or onto bread rounds.

## Creamed Corned Beef Bites

4½ *-ounce can corned beef spread*
  4  *ounces cream cheese*
  1  *teaspoon prepared mustard*
  1  *tablespoon horseradish*
  6  *slices firm rye bread*

**1**   Thoroughly mix corned beef, cheese, mustard and horseradish. Refrigerate for about 1½ hours.

**2**   Using a 1½-inch round biscuit cutter, cut out 4 rounds of bread from each slice.

**3**   Fill gun with corned beef mixture. Fit with decorator tip.

**4**   Using gun at high speed, pipe decorative mounds onto bread rounds. Refrigerate.

**5**   Serve at room temperature.

Makes 18 to 24 canapés.

———

*Variation:* Corned beef mixture may be piped into raw zucchini. Cut zucchini in half lengthwise and remove seeds. Then slice into ¾- to 1-inch sections; fill with mixture.

*Shown left, on a variety of pastry shells and puffs: Olive Cheese Pastries (p. 67), Curried Chicken (p. 54), Greek Spinach and Feta Boats (p. 51), Russian Coulibiac Tarts (p. 48), Italian Sausage and Peppers (p. 50).*

## Liver Pâté
## Pie

Well worth the effort! Truly the best pâté we've ever had.

9-inch baked Pie Shell (see recipe, page 118)
1 cup plus 1 tablespoon butter
1 large onion, finely chopped
4 shallots, finely chopped
1 tart, medium apple, peeled, cored and diced
1½ pounds chicken livers, cleaned
⅓ cup heavy cream
2 teaspoons lemon juice
1½ tablespoons brandy
1½ teaspoons salt
Pepper to taste
¼ cup coarsely chopped salted pistachio nuts

1   Prepare baked Pie Shell as directed.

2   Melt 3 tablespoons butter in fry pan. Add onion and shallots; sauté about 10 minutes, until soft. Add apple; cook 3 to 4 minutes more. Remove to electric blender and whirl. Leave puréed mixture in blender.

3   Melt 4 tablespoons butter in large fry pan. Cut livers in half; cook in fry pan over medium high heat for about 6 minutes, turning once or twice. Do not crowd the pan. (Cook livers in 2 batches if necessary.) Livers should be browned outside and just slightly pink inside. Remove to a plate. Reserve pan juices.

4   Add a few livers to the onion apple purée in the blender; whirl on medium to high speed. Remove to a bowl.

5   In blender, mix remaining livers with pan juices, heavy cream, lemon juice and brandy. This will have to be done in stages, adding a few livers and some of the liquids to the blender at a time.

6   Transfer mixture to bowl containing purée. Using a wooden spoon, push mixture through a sieve or strainer. Add salt and pepper. Cool completely.

7   Cream remaining 10 tablespoons of butter; beat into the cooled liver mixture. Reserve 1 cup of mixture for garnish.

8   Place balance of pâté in baked Pie Shell, smoothing top with rubber spatula so it is absolutely flat.

9   Fill gun with reserved pâté. Fit with decorator tip.

10   Using gun at high speed, pipe S-shaped squiggles around outer edge of pie. Sprinkle pistachio nuts over undecorated area. Refrigerate.

Makes 16 to 18 hors d'oeuvres or 10 appetizer servings.

# Hot Hors d'oeuvres

# Hot Hors d'oeuvres

Want a really warm way to welcome your friends? Experienced party-givers know that hot hors d'oeuvres are among the best ice-breakers ever invented. They're versatile, too, since many hors d'oeuvre mixtures also make excellent main courses and side dishes. Eggplant and Clams, presented here as an hors d'oeuvre, can also be served over pasta as a main dish at lunch or dinner. Similarly, Mushroom Clouds, a delicious canapé, can double as a vegetable accompaniment to roast lamb or beef. Or try it in reverse. Shrimp Newburg, Chicken Tetrazzinis, and Tarragon Chicken and Mushrooms, normally served as main courses, can easily be transformed into tasty, unusual hors d'oeuvres — a new use for dependable old recipes. There's no limit to the kinds of treats that can grace an hors d'oeuvre table, so feel free to experiment.

Preparing Ahead: As a general rule, the foods in this section may be prepared a day or two in advance and stored in the refrigerator. Heat them in the oven or broiler just before serving. (For more specific directions, see "Filled Toast Cups and Tartlette Shells" on page 43, "Fried Puffs, Flutes and Fingers" on page 56 and "Hot Cheese Cookies" on page 67.)

## Polish Sausage Biscuits

½  pound precooked Kielbasa sausage
1¾  cups all-purpose flour
2½  teaspoons double acting baking
     powder
1¼  teaspoons salt
  4  tablespoons butter
  1  teaspoon dried instant minced onions
  1  cup milk
     Prepared mustard (optional)

**1**  Remove casing from sausage with small, sharp knife. Press sausage through fine blade of a meat grinder into a bowl. Set aside.

**2**  Mix together flour, baking powder and salt in a large bowl. Add butter; blend together with fingers or pastry blender until mixture resembles coarse corn meal. Do not overblend. Add onions; stir.

**3**  Add ground sausage and milk to flour mixture. Stir vigorously with a wooden spoon just until ingredients are blended.

**4**  Fill gun with mixture. Fit with decorator tip.

**5**  Using gun at high speed, pipe small mounds 1 inch in diameter onto a greased baking sheet, about 1 inch apart. Brush tops with mustard.

**6**  Place in preheated 425-degree oven for 15 minutes, until lightly browned. Serve hot.

Makes 5 to 6 dozen hors d'oeuvres.

## Bacon Stuffed Mushrooms

12  slices bacon
  1  pound medium mushrooms (about 36)
  1  cup finely chopped onions
⅔  cup finely chopped celery
½  cup chicken broth
  2  tablespoons butter
     Pinch of powdered thyme, rosemary
       and sage
½  cup packaged bread crumbs
     Salt and pepper to taste

**1**  Fry bacon until crisp. Drain on paper towels. Reserve 4 tablespoons bacon drippings.

**2**  Remove mushroom stems and chop until fine. Reserve mushroom caps.

**3**  Heat reserved bacon drippings in fry pan. Add chopped mushroom stems, onions and celery. Sauté for 15 minutes. Add broth, butter, thyme, rosemary and sage; heat until butter is melted. Remove from heat.

**4**  Crumble bacon well with fingers until pieces are smaller than grains of rice. Add bacon bits and bread crumbs to mixture; stir well. Taste; add salt and pepper as needed.

**5**  Fill gun with bacon mixture. Fit with decorator tip.

**6**  Place reserved mushroom caps in baking pan. Using gun at high speed, pipe mixture into caps.

**7**  Broil in preheated broiler for 5 to 7 minutes until mixture is toasty and mushrooms are very hot.

Makes 3 dozen hors d'oeuvres.

# Mushroom Clouds

Puffs of pastry, light as air, with succulent mushroomy centers . . . these clouds are heavenly.

6 *tablespoons butter*

2 *cups very finely chopped onions*

2 *pounds mushrooms*

1 *tablespoon lemon juice*

¼ *teaspoon dried dill weed*

1 *teaspoon salt*

6 *tablespoons all-purpose flour*

½ *cup sour cream*

   *Pâte à Choux miniature cream puffs (see recipe, page 57)*

**1**   Melt butter in large saucepan. Add onions; sauté for 15 minutes.

**2**   Meanwhile, chop mushrooms until fine. (It's helpful when chopping a large quantity of mushrooms to use a single- or double-bladed metal chopper in a wooden bowl.) Add to pan with onions; cook and stir over medium heat for 10 minutes.

**3**   Drain mixture in small-holed colander; return to saucepan. Stir in lemon juice, dill weed and salt. Reheat on low heat. Sprinkle flour over mixture and stir. Add sour cream; cook, stirring, for another 3 minutes. Remove from heat. Cover with plastic wrap. Set aside to cool.

**4**   Prepare Pâte à Choux miniature cream puffs as directed.

**5**   Place puffs on lightly greased baking sheets. Cut the cap off each puff. Reserve caps.

**6**   Fill gun with mushroom mixture. Fit with decorator tip.

**7**   Using gun at high speed, pipe mixture into cream puffs. Cover each puff with a reserved cap.

**8**   Bake in preheated 350-degree oven for 15 minutes, until very hot.

Makes 5 to 6 dozen hors d'oeuvres.

---

*Variation:* Mushroom Clouds may be served as a vegetable course accompanying roast lamb or beef.

# Rice
# Torta

A dandy Italian treat.

*10-ounce package frozen chopped
    spinach, cooked*

  *3  cups cooked rice*

*15-ounce container ricotta cheese*

  *1  cup grated Parmesan cheese*

  *¼  teaspoon salt*

  *⅛  teaspoon pepper*

  *4  large eggs*
    *Olive oil*
    *Packaged bread crumbs*

**1**   Drain spinach and squeeze out excess water. Place in bowl with rice, 1 cup of ricotta, Parmesan, salt and pepper. Mix well.

**2**   Beat 3 of the eggs and fold into rice mixture.

**3**   Grease a 9x9-inch baking pan with olive oil; coat with bread crumbs. Spoon rice mixture into pan.

**4**   Beat remaining egg and brush on top of mixture.

**5**   Bake in preheated 350-degree oven for 30 minutes, until firm. Cut into 36 squares; remove to a serving platter.

**6**   Fill gun with remaining ricotta. Fit with decorator tip.

**7**   Using gun at high speed, pipe a ricotta kiss on each square. Serve warm.

Makes 36 hors d'oeuvres.

# Roquefort
# Burgerettes

  *1  pound lean ground beef*

  *1  large egg*

  *1  teaspoon salt*

*¼  teaspoon pepper*

  *2  tablespoons grated onion*

  *7  slices firm white bread, toasted*
    *Roquefort Topping (recipe follows)*

**1**   Mix beef, egg, salt, pepper and onion together. Shape into 28 balls.

**2**   Using a 1½-inch round biscuit cutter, cut 4 rounds from each slice of toast.

**3**   Place the beef balls on the toast and flatten, forming mini-burgers slightly larger than the toast rounds. Place on baking pan and broil in preheated broiler for 3 to 4 minutes.

**4**   Fill gun with Roquefort Topping. Fit with decorator tip.

**5**   Using gun at high speed, pipe a quick Roquefort kiss on each burger. Serve hot.

Makes 28 hors d'oeuvres.

### Roquefort Topping

*¼  pound Roquefort or blue cheese,
    softened*

  *1  tablespoon butter, softened*

Using a wooden spoon, press cheese through strainer into a bowl. Add butter and mix thoroughly.

## Moussaka Squares

¾  cup plus 3 tablespoons vegetable oil

3  1-pound eggplants, peeled and sliced
   ⅛ to ¼ inch thick

2  cups chopped onions

2  pounds ground beef

2  tablespoons tomato paste

½  cup red wine

¼  cup chopped parsley

1  teaspoon salt

¼  teaspoon pepper

   Pinch of cinnamon

   Pinch of rosemary

½  cup packaged bread crumbs

½  cup grated Parmesan cheese

   Ricotta Sauce (recipe follows)

1  cup ricotta cheese

**1**  Brown eggplant slices on both sides. Do it in batches, using 2 tablespoons oil per batch. Set aside.

**2**  If all the oil has been used up, add 3 more tablespoons to pan. Add onions and sauté for 15 minutes.

**3**  Add beef, breaking it up in the pan. Stir and brown for about 10 minutes. Add tomato paste, wine, parsley, salt, pepper, cinnamon and rosemary. Stir well. Simmer until liquid is absorbed. Remove from heat.

**4**  Grease two 9x9-inch baking pans. Sprinkle the bottoms lightly with some of the bread crumbs. Arrange alternate layers of eggplant and meat, beginning with eggplant. Sprinkle each layer with Parmesan and bread crumbs.

**5**  Pour Ricotta Sauce over top. Bake in preheated 375-degree oven for 40 minutes until top is golden. Cool on wire rack for about 30 minutes.

**6**  Cut each moussaka into 36 squares. Remove squares carefully—inverting them so sauce is on the bottom—and put them into small paper muffin cups on a serving platter.

**7**  Fill gun with ricotta cheese. Fit with decorator tip.

**8**  Using gun at high speed, pipe a ricotta rosette on each moussaka square. Serve warm.

Makes 6 dozen hors d'oeuvres.

———

*Variation:* To serve as a main course, cut each pan of moussaka into 6 servings, but do not invert. Remove to serving platter and pipe ricotta on each serving.

### Ricotta Sauce

6  tablespoons butter

5  tablespoons all-purpose flour

3  cups milk

3  eggs, well beaten

2  cups ricotta cheese

   Pinch of nutmeg

**1**  Melt butter in saucepan. Blend in flour with a wire whisk.

**2**  Stir in milk gradually. Cook, stirring constantly, until thick and smooth; remove from heat.

**3**  Stir a small amount of hot mixture into beaten eggs. Combine egg mixture with contents of saucepan, stirring well. Stir in ricotta and nutmeg.

# Noodle Pudding Nuggets

These nuggets are a nice way to use your noodles.

  8 ounces cottage cheese

  8 ounces cream cheese

¼ cup granulated sugar

  3 large eggs

20-ounce can crushed pineapple, drained

  2 teaspoons vanilla extract

½ teaspoon salt

  8-ounce package ¼ -inch-wide egg
       noodles

  8-ounce container ricotta cheese

**1** Place cottage and cream cheeses in large bowl. With beater at medium to high speed, cream the cheeses. Add sugar and eggs; beat well. Stir in pineapple, vanilla and salt.

**2** Cook noodles according to package directions; drain well. Mix thoroughly with cheese egg mixture.

**3** Grease a 9x13-inch baking pan. Pour in noodle mixture and distribute evenly.

**4** Bake in preheated 350-degree oven 50 to 60 minutes until a sharp knife inserted in center comes out clean. Remove from oven; cool on wire rack for 20 to 30 minutes.

**5** Using a sharp knife, cut very carefully into 60 squares.

**6** Place small paper muffin cup liners on serving platter and fill each with a noodle square.

**7** Fill gun with ricotta. Fit with decorator tip.

**8** Using gun at high speed, pipe a ricotta rosette on each square. Serve warm or at room temperature.

Makes 60 hors d'oeuvres.

———

*Variation:* To serve noodle pudding as a side dish, bake as directed. Pipe ricotta over top in decorative swirls. Cut into larger serving portions.

## Onion
## Cheese Tart

Golden onions in sherried sour cream
on a cheddar cheesy crust.

*Cheddar Crust (recipe follows)*
¼  cup butter
 4  cups thinly sliced and quartered onions
 3  large eggs
 1  cup sour cream
 2  tablespoons sherry
½  teaspoon salt
⅛  teaspoon pepper
    Pinch of nutmeg
 2  slices bacon, cut into 1-inch squares

**1**   Prepare Cheddar Crust as directed.

**2**   Melt butter in saucepan. Add onions;
sauté until golden and tender. Remove
from heat and cool.

**3**   Beat eggs. Add sour cream, sherry,
salt, pepper and nutmeg; mix thoroughly.

**4**   Add onions to sour cream mixture.
Taste for seasoning.

**5**   Fill Cheddar Crust with mixture; top
with bacon squares.

**6**   Place pie plate on baking pan to catch
drippings. Bake in preheated 350-degree
oven for 40 minutes.

**7**   Fill gun with dough reserved from
Cheddar Crust. Fit with decorator tip.

**8**   Remove onion tart from oven. Using
gun at low speed, pipe a lattice topping
over surface (five rows down and five
rows across). Replace in oven and bake
another 15 minutes.

10 hors d'oeuvre servings or 8 appetizer
servings.

### Cheddar Crust

¾  pound sharp Cheddar cheese, grated
 6  tablespoons softened butter
¼  teaspoon salt
 1  tablespoon caraway seeds
¾  cup all-purpose flour
 1  egg, slightly beaten

**1**   Place all ingredients in bowl; blend
together using fingers or pastry blender.

**2**   Gather together into a ball. Knead
well. Reserve 1 cup of dough for lattice
topping (keep at room temperature).

**3**   Press balance of dough into 9-inch pie
plate, distributing evenly along bottom
and sides. Refrigerate until ready to fill.

## Filled Toast Cups and Tartlette Shells

*Every well-stocked freezer should have a good supply of these great little entertainers. You can make them whenever you have a little time (and that's all it takes), and freeze them to use as needed. However, it's best to freeze the cups and shells separately from the fillings. Thaw, fill and heat on the day of serving.*

*These fillings are all eminently freeze-able:*
*Arroz con Pollo*
*Beef and Pasta*
*Beef with Bearnaise*
*Chicken Tetrazzinis*
*Chili con Carne*
*Curried Chicken*
*Curried Shrimp*
*Greek Spinach and Feta Boats*
*Ham and Cheese au Gratin*
*Italian Sausage and Peppers*
*Kasha and Beef*
*Mexican Chicken*
*Sausage and Leek Pies*
*Shrimp Newburg*
*Tarragon Chicken and Mushrooms*

*Other fillings can be prepared a day or two in advance and refrigerated. Shortly before serving, pipe the fillings into the shells or cups with your electric foodgun, pop them into the oven — and serve them piping hot.*

# Toast Cups

*1 loaf diet thin white bread*
*(30 slices per pound)*
*Melted butter*

**1**   Using a 2- or 2½-inch biscuit cutter, cut out one bread round from each slice of bread. (Leftover bread can be made into bread crumbs and saved for other recipes.)

**2**   Line miniature muffin tins with bread rounds.

**3**   Brush the insides of the bread cups with melted butter.

**4**   Bake in preheated 350-degree oven for about 10 minutes, until golden brown. Do not overbake. Remove from muffin tins and cool on wire rack.

Makes 28 toast cups.

*Variation:* Whole wheat diet thin bread may be used to make whole wheat toast cups.

## Pastry
## Tartlette Shells

1  cup butter, softened
8-ounce package cream cheese
2½  cups all-purpose flour

**1**   Place all ingredients in a bowl; blend together using fingers or fork.

**2**   Gather pastry together and knead for about 30 seconds. Form into a flattened ball and divide into 4 equal parts. Completely cover each part with plastic wrap and refrigerate for at least 1 hour.

**3**   Remove one quarter at a time from refrigerator. Cut into 16 to 18 equal pieces. Roll into balls and place in tartlette pans measuring 1 inch across bottom and 2 inches across top. Press dough firmly, distributing evenly over bottom and sides of pan. Break off any excess extending out of the pan. Repeat with each quarter.

**4**   To make sure dough remains flat, press aluminum foil down on top of it. Fill with uncooked rice or beans.

**5**   Bake in preheated 400-degree oven for about 7 minutes, until pastry starts to take on some color. Remove from pans and cool on wire rack.

Makes about 6 dozen tartlette shells.

## Kasha
## and Beef

Hearty party fare.

3  tablespoons vegetable oil
1½  cups chopped onions
½  pound ground beef
2½  cups chicken broth
⅔  cup kasha (medium roasted buck-
    wheat groats)
3  tablespoons egg pastina, cooked
    Salt and pepper
    Toast Cups (see recipe, page 43)

**1**   Heat oil in fry pan. Add onions; sauté until soft and golden. Add beef; cook over medium high heat, stirring often, until well done.

**2**   Remove to electric blender. Add ½ cup of broth; whirl until there are no big pieces of meat. Remove to bowl.

**3**   Heat remaining two cups of broth in fry pan. Add kasha; cover and cook over medium low heat for about 10 minutes until broth is absorbed.

**4**   Add kasha and pastina to beef mixture; stir. Add salt and pepper to taste.

**5**   Fill gun with mixture. Fit with decorator tip.

**6**   Place Toast Cups on baking sheet. Using gun at high speed, pipe mixture into cups.

**7**   Bake in preheated 350-degree oven for 10 minutes, until very hot.

Makes 4 to 5 dozen hors d'oeuvres.

# Beef
# with Bearnaise

Aromatic French saucery . . . spells the difference between plain beef and fancy fare.

2 *tablespoons vegetable oil*

1 *pound ground beef*

½ *cup chicken broth*

2 *tablespoons white wine*

1 *tablespoon tarragon vinegar*

1 *tablespoon grated onion*

1 *teaspoon dried tarragon leaves*

3 *egg yolks*

2 *tablespoons lemon juice*

¼ *teaspoon salt*

⅛ *teaspoon pepper*

½ *cup butter*

 *Toast Cups or Pastry Tartlette Shells (see recipes, pages 43, 44)*

**1**   Heat oil in fry pan. Add beef; cook over medium high heat, stirring often, until well done. Drain well.

**2**   Remove to electric blender. Add broth and whirl until there are no big pieces of meat. Place in bowl and set aside.

**3**   Place wine, vinegar, onion and tarragon in a small fry pan. Bring to a boil; cook until almost all liquid disappears. Remove to electric blender container.

**4**   Add egg yolks, lemon juice, salt and pepper. Whirl on low speed.

**5**   Melt butter in saucepan until hot and bubbly. Add very slowly to blender, whirling until the sauce is thick and smooth and has consistency of mayonnaise.

**6**   Add sauce to beef; stir well.

**7**   Fill gun with mixture. Fit with decorator tip.

**8**   Place Toast Cups or Pastry Shells on baking sheet. Using gun at high speed, pipe mixture into cups.

**9**   Bake in preheated 350-degree oven for 15 minutes, until very hot.

Makes 4 to 5 dozen hors d'oeuvres.

*Variation:* Cooked chicken or cooked shrimp may be substituted for beef—but these should be put through a meat grinder rather than an electric blender.

## Beef
## and Pasta

1   tablespoon vegetable oil

½   pound ground beef

8-ounce can tomato sauce

2   tablespoons grated Parmesan cheese

½   cup egg pastina, cooked

½   teaspoon salt

Toast Cups (see recipe, page 43)

Additional grated Parmesan cheese

**1**   Heat oil in fry pan. Add beef; cook, stirring often, until well done. Drain well.

**2**   Remove to electric blender. Add tomato sauce and whirl until there are no big pieces of meat. Remove to bowl.

**3**   Add cheese, pastina and salt. Mix thoroughly.

**4**   Fill gun with mixture. Fit with decorator tip.

**5**   Place Toast Cups on baking sheet. Using gun at high speed, pipe mixture into cups; sprinkle with additional cheese.

**6**   Bake in preheated 350-degree oven for 10 minutes, until very hot.

Makes about 4 dozen hors d'oeuvres.

## Chili
## con Carne

Immensely satisfying mini-morsels of smoothly-sauced beef and beans.

2   tablespoons cooking oil

½   cup chopped onions

¼   cup chopped green peppers

1   clove garlic, chopped

½   pound ground beef

1   cup canned tomatoes

1   tablespoon chili powder

½   teaspoon powdered cumin

½   teaspoon oregano

½   teaspoon salt

1   cup canned kidney beans, drained

Toast Cups (see recipe, page 43)

**1**   Heat oil in large fry pan. Sauté onions, green pepper and garlic for 10 minutes. Add beef. Cook over medium high heat, stirring occasionally, until thoroughly browned. Add tomatoes and seasonings; simmer for 10 minutes.

**2**   Remove mixture to electric blender container. Add beans; whirl until there are no big pieces. (This will have to be done in batches.) Remove to bowl and mix thoroughly.

**3**   Fill gun with mixture. Fit with decorator tip.

**4**   Place Toast Cups on baking sheet. Using gun at high speed, pipe mixture into cups.

**5**   Bake in preheated 350-degree oven for 15 minutes, until very hot.

Makes about 4 dozen hors d'oeuvres.

## Eggplant and Clams

1 medium eggplant (about 1 pound)
1 tablespoon butter
½ cup chopped onions
2 cloves garlic, chopped
2 8-ounce cans minced clams
¼ cup heavy cream
1 tablespoon lemon juice
¼ cup chopped parsley
   Salt and pepper
2 tablespoons packaged bread crumbs
   Toast Cups (see recipe, page 43)

**1**  Peel and dice eggplant. Place in boiling water to cover; boil for 5 to 10 minutes, until tender. Drain in colander. Set aside to cool.

**2**  Heat butter in fry pan. Add onions and garlic; sauté for about 7 minutes. Remove to electric blender container.

**3**  Drain clams, reserving ¼ cup of liquid. Add clams, heavy cream, lemon juice and reserved clam liquid to mixture in blender. Whirl until there are no big pieces. Remove to bowl.

**4**  Thoroughly squeeze all water out of eggplant. Mash with a fork and add to clam mixture. Mix in parsley, salt and pepper to taste, and bread crumbs.

**5**  Fill gun with eggplant and clam mixture. Fit with decorator tip.

**6**  Place Toast Cups on baking sheet. Using gun at high speed, pipe mixture into cups.

**7**  Bake in preheated 350-degree oven for 15 minutes, until very hot.

Makes about 4 dozen hors d'oeuvres.

## Eggs Florentine

8 hard-cooked eggs, shelled
½ of a 10-ounce package frozen chopped
   spinach, cooked and well drained
2 tablespoons grated onions
1 tablespoon plus 1 teaspoon Dijon
   mustard
1 teaspoon salt
⅛ teaspoon pepper
½ cup mayonnaise
   Toast Cups or Pastry Tartlette Shells
   (see recipes, pages 43, 44)

**1**  Mash eggs in a bowl until quite fine. (This is easily done with a potato masher that has metal squares on the bottom.)

**2**  Add spinach, onion, mustard, seasonings and mayonnaise to eggs. Mix well.

**3**  Fill gun with mixture. Fit with decorator tip.

**4**  Place Toast Cups or Pastry Shells on baking sheet. Using gun at high speed, pipe mixture into shells.

**5**  Bake in preheated 350-degree oven for 15 minutes, until very hot.

Makes 4 to 5 dozen hors d'oeuvres.

## Russian Coulibiac Tarts

Toast cups filled with a piping hot mixture featuring salmon and cream cheese.

¼  cup rice
 1  tablespoon butter
½  cup finely chopped onions
 8  ounces cream cheese
¼  pound smoked salmon, very finely diced
 1  teaspoon snipped dill
 1  hard-cooked egg, finely chopped
    Toast Cups (see recipe, page 43)

**1**   Cook rice in boiling water until tender. Set aside to cool.

**2**   Melt butter in fry pan; sauté onions for 10 minutes. Cool.

**3**   Place cream cheese in a bowl and soften with a wooden spoon.

**4**   Add salmon, dill and egg to cream cheese; mix well. Add cooled rice and onions; mix thoroughly.

**5**   Fill gun with smoked salmon mixture. Fit with decorator tip.

**6**   Place Toast Cups on baking sheet. Using gun at high speed, pipe mixture into cups.

**7**   Bake in preheated 350-degree oven for 15 minutes, or until very hot.

Makes about 4 dozen hors d'oeuvres.

## Broccoli Cheddar Tarts

 1  bunch broccoli, cooked
 3  tablespoons butter
¼  cup all-purpose flour
⅔  cup chicken broth
1½  cups grated sharp Cheddar cheese
 1  teaspoon salt
    Pepper to taste
    Toast Cups or Pastry Tartlette Shells (see recipes, pages 43, 44)

**1**   Press broccoli through the fine blade of a meat grinder into a bowl. Drain; set aside.

**2**   Heat butter in saucepan. Add flour; stir with a wire whisk. Add broth; stir until hot, thickened and smooth. Add cheese, salt and pepper; stir over low heat until cheese melts and sauce is smooth and quite thick. Remove from heat.

**3**   Add broccoli and mix well. Set aside to cool.

**4**   Fill gun with cooled mixture. Fit with decorator tip.

**5**   Place Toast Cups or Pastry Shells on baking sheets. Using gun at high speed, pipe mixture into cups.

**6**   Bake in preheated 350-degree oven for 15 minutes, until very hot.

Makes about 5 dozen hors d'oeuvres.

## Swiss Tuna Tarts

7-ounce can tuna fish, drained
½  cup grated Swiss cheese
1½  tablespoons lemon juice
½  cup heavy cream
1  egg, well beaten
2  tablespoons grated onion
½  teaspoon salt
⅛  teaspoon pepper
   Toast Cups or Pastry Tartlette Shells
      (see recipes, pages 43, 44)

**1**   Place tuna in bowl. Using fingers, flake very well until there are no chunks. Set aside.

**2**   Grate cheese until fine in electric blender or Mouli grater. Add to tuna fish. Mix in lemon juice, heavy cream, egg, onion, salt and pepper.

**3**   Fill gun with mixture. Fit with decorator tip.

**4**   Place Toast Cups or Pastry Shells on baking sheet. Using gun at high speed, pipe mixture into cups.

**5**   Bake in preheated 350-degree oven for 15 minutes, until very hot.

Makes 3 to 4 dozen hors d'oeuvres.

## Ham and Cheese au Gratin

Ham and Swiss cheese have been going steady for years. Here they make a great appetizer.

½  pound boiled ham
½  pound Swiss cheese, cubed
2  large eggs, lightly beaten
1½  cups heavy cream
1  teaspoon salt
⅛  teaspoon garlic powder
⅛  teaspoon pepper
   Whole Wheat Toast Cups or Pastry
      Tartlette Shells (see recipes,
      pages 43, 44)
   Packaged bread crumbs

**1**   Press ham through fine blade of meat grinder into bowl.

**2**   Grate cheese in electric blender or Mouli grater. Add to ground ham. Stir in eggs, heavy cream, salt, garlic and pepper.

**3**   Fill gun with mixture. Fit with decorator tip.

**4**   Using gun at high speed, pipe mixture into Whole Wheat Toast Cups. Sprinkle with bread crumbs. Place on baking pans.

**5**   Bake in preheated 350-degree oven for 15 minutes, until very hot.

Makes 6 to 7 dozen hors d'oeuvres.

## Italian Sausage and Peppers

1 *pound Italian sweet sausage*
2 *tablespoons cooking oil*
2 *cups chopped green peppers*
1 *tablespoon all-purpose flour*
½ *cup chicken broth*
½ *cup tomato sauce*
*Toast Cups (see recipe, page 43)*

**1** Remove casings from sausage with a small sharp knife. In a fry pan, break up sausage meat with a fork and cook over medium low heat, stirring often, until well done. Remove to electric blender container.

**2** Heat oil in fry pan. Add green peppers; sauté for 15 minutes. Blend in flour. Add broth and tomato sauce, stirring until smooth and thickened. Remove from heat.

**3** Add green pepper mixture to sausage in blender; whirl until there are no big pieces. (This may have to be done in batches.) Remove to bowl and stir.

**4** Fill gun with mixture. Fit with decorator tip.

**5** Place Toast Cups on baking sheet. Using gun at high speed, pipe mixture into cups.

**6** Bake in preheated 350-degree oven for 15 minutes, until very hot.

Makes about 4 dozen hors d'oeuvres.

## Sausage and Leek Pies

16-*ounce package sausage meat*
2 *large leeks*
½ *cup chicken broth*
⅓ *cup heavy cream*
*Toast Cups or Pastry Tartlette Shells (see recipes, pages 43, 44)*

**1** In a fry pan, break up sausage meat with a fork and brown evenly over medium low heat until well done. Follow package directions for cooking time. Remove from heat.

**2** Cut off green tops of leeks. Trim roots; wash well. Slice roots into thin rounds and add to chicken broth. Boil for about 5 minutes, until tender. Remove mixture to electric blender container.

**3** Add sausage and heavy cream to blender. Whirl until there are no big pieces. (This may have to be done in batches.) Remove to bowl and mix well. Cool.

**4** Fill gun with mixture. Fit with decorator tip.

**5** Place Toast Cups or Pastry Shells on baking sheet. Using gun at high speed, pipe mixture into cups.

**6** Bake in preheated 350-degree oven for 15 minutes, until very hot.

Makes 3 to 4 dozen hors d'oeuvres.

# Greek Spinach and Feta Boats

When a Greek classic turns into a contemporary conversation piece, the cook turns into a legend.

1  tablespoon butter

½  cup grated onions

8  ounces feta cheese

8  ounces large curd creamed cottage cheese

4  scallions, finely chopped

1  tablespoon finely chopped parsley

2  teaspoons finely snipped dill

10-ounce package frozen chopped spinach, cooked and well drained

½  teaspoon salt

Pepper to taste

Pinch of nutmeg

2  eggs, well beaten

Pastry Tartlette Shells (see recipe, page 44)

**1**  Melt butter in fry pan. Add onion and cook for 5 minutes. Cool.

**2**  Place feta cheese in a bowl. Using fork or fingers, break up cheese until it is fine and crumbly. Add onions and all other ingredients except Pastry Shells. Mix well.

**3**  Fill gun with spinach feta mixture. Fit with decorator tip.

**4**  Place Pastry Tartlette Shells on baking sheet. Using gun at high speed, pipe mixture into shells.

**5**  Bake in preheated 350-degree oven for 15 minutes, until very hot.

Makes 4 to 5 dozen hors d'oeuvres.

———

*Variation:* Fill raw mushroom caps with spinach and feta mixture. Place on greased baking pan and bake in preheated 350-degree oven for 15 minutes. Makes about 6 dozen filled mushrooms. They're great for dieters—about 10 calories each.

## Spinach and Tuna

Tuna fish and spinach in a lemon-creamy combination.

7-ounce can tuna fish, drained
½ of a 10-ounce package frozen chopped spinach, cooked and well drained
2 teaspoons lemon juice
½ cup mayonnaise
¼ teaspoon salt
Pepper to taste
Toast Cups, white or whole wheat (see recipe, page 43)

**1** Place tuna fish in a bowl. Using fingers, flake very well until there are no chunks. Add spinach, lemon juice, mayonnaise, salt and pepper. Mix well.

**2** Fill gun with mixture. Fit with decorator tip.

**3** Place Toast Cups on baking sheet. Using gun at high speed, pipe mixture into cups.

**4** Bake in preheated 350-degree oven for 15 minutes, until very hot.

Makes 3 to 4 dozen hors d'oeuvres.

## Shrimp Newburg

2 tablespoons butter
½ pound mushrooms, sliced
2 cups cooked shrimp
⅔ cup heavy cream
1 tablespoon sherry
1 egg yolk
Salt and pepper
Toast Cups or Pastry Tartlette Shells (see recipes, pages 43, 44)

**1** Melt butter in fry pan and sauté mushrooms for 7 minutes. Drain liquid.

**2** Press mushrooms and shrimp through the fine blade of a meat grinder into a bowl. Add cream, sherry, egg yolk, salt and pepper to taste. Mix well.

**3** Fill gun with mixture. Fit with decorator tip.

**4** Place Toast Cups or Tartlette Shells on baking sheet. Using gun at high speed, pipe mixture into shells.

**5** Bake in preheated 350-degree oven for 15 minutes, until very hot.

Makes 3 to 4 dozen hors d'oeuvres.

## Curried Shrimp

 4 tablespoons butter
½ cup chopped onions
¼ cup chopped green pepper
¼ cup chopped, pared carrots
¼ cup chopped celery
1½ cups cooked shrimp
 1 tablespoon all-purpose flour
¾ cup chicken broth
 1 tablespoon curry powder
 Salt
 Toast Cups or Pastry Tartlette Shells
 (see recipes, pages 43, 44)
 Chopped salted peanuts

**1** Melt 3 tablespoons of butter in fry pan. Add onions, green pepper, carrots and celery. Sauté for 10 minutes.

**2** Press sautéed mixture and shrimp through the fine blade of a meat grinder into bowl.

**3** Melt remaining tablespoon of butter in saucepan; blend in flour. Add broth; heat, stirring, until sauce is thickened and smooth. Add curry powder; stir. Remove from heat.

**4** Stir sauce and shrimp mixture together. Add salt to taste.

**5** Fill gun with curried shrimp. Fit with decorator tip.

**6** Place Toast Cups or Pastry Shells on baking sheet. Using gun at high speed, pipe mixture into cups. Sprinkle with nuts.

**7** Bake in preheated 350-degree oven for 15 minutes, until very hot.

Makes about 4 dozen hors d'oeuvres.

## Tarragon Chicken and Mushrooms

1¼ cups cooked chicken
 3 tablespoons butter
½ pound mushrooms, very finely
 chopped
¼ cup grated onions
 1 tablespoon lemon juice
¼ teaspoon dried tarragon leaves
¼ cup dry white wine
¼ cup heavy cream
¾ teaspoon salt
⅛ teaspoon pepper
 Toast Cups or Pastry Tartlette Shells
 (see recipes, pages 43, 44)

**1** Press chicken through fine blade of a meat grinder into a bowl. Set aside.

**2** Melt butter in fry pan. Add mushrooms, onions, lemon juice and tarragon; sauté for 5 minutes. Stir in wine; cook for 3 minutes more over medium high heat.

**3** Add mushroom mixture to chicken. Stir in heavy cream, salt and pepper.

**4** Fill gun with mixture. Fit with decorator tip.

**5** Place Toast Cups or Pastry Shells on baking sheet. Using gun at high speed, pipe mixture into cups.

**6** Bake in preheated 350-degree oven for 15 minutes, until very hot.

Makes 3 dozen hors d'oeuvres.

## Curried Chicken

Always a social success . . . because to curry chicken is to curry favor with your family and guests.

2 cups cooked chicken
3 tablespoons butter
1 cup chopped onions
½ cup chopped green pepper
1 apple, pared, cored and diced
¾ cup chicken broth
4 teaspoons curry powder
1 teaspoon salt
⅛ teaspoon pepper
⅓ cup heavy cream
　Toast Cups or Pastry Tartlette Shells
　　(see recipes, pages 43, 44)
　Toasted coconut

**1** Press chicken through fine blade of a meat grinder into a bowl. Set aside.

**2** Heat butter in fry pan. Add onions and green pepper; sauté for 10 minutes. Add apple; cook for another 5 minutes, until apple is tender.

**3** Add broth, curry powder, salt and pepper to pan. Cook over low heat for 5 minutes. Remove from heat. Add heavy cream.

**4** Place in electric blender and whirl until there are no big pieces. Add to bowl with chicken; mix well.

**5** Fill gun with curried chicken mixture. Fit with decorator tip.

**6** Place Toast Cups or Pastry Shells on baking sheets. Using gun at high speed, pipe mixture into cups; sprinkle a little coconut over each.

**7** Bake in preheated 350-degree oven for 15 minutes, until very hot.

Makes 4 to 5 dozen hors d'oeuvres.

## Arroz con Pollo

1½  cups cooked chicken
 1  tablespoon butter
½  cup chopped onions
 1  clove garlic, chopped
17-ounce can tomatoes
¼  teaspoon oregano
⅛  teaspoon saffron
½  teaspoon salt
½  cup chicken broth
½  cup rice
     Toast Cups (see recipe, page 43)

**1**  Press chicken through fine blade of a meat grinder into bowl. Set aside.

**2**  Melt butter in fry pan. Add onions and garlic; sauté for 10 minutes. Add tomatoes, seasonings, broth and rice. Bring to a boil; cover and simmer for 15 minutes.

**3**  Place contents of pan in electric blender; whirl until there are no big pieces.

**4**  Add rice mixture to chicken; stir thoroughly.

**5**  Fill gun with mixture. Fit with decorator tip.

**6**  Place Toast Cups on baking sheet. Using gun at high speed, pipe mixture into cups.

**7**  Bake in preheated 350-degree oven for 10 minutes, until very hot.

Makes 5 to 6 dozen hors d'oeuvres.

## Mexican Chicken

A south-of-the-border specialty that will win olés.

1½  cups cooked chicken
¾  cup pitted black olives
 3  tablespoons butter
 1  cup chopped onions
 1  clove garlic, chopped
 1  cup chopped green pepper
 1  teaspoon salt
     Pepper to taste
17-ounce can tomatoes
     Toast Cups (see recipe, page 43)
½  pound bacon, fried and crumbled

**1**  Press chicken and olives through fine blade of a meat grinder into bowl. Set aside.

**2**  Melt butter in large fry pan. Add onions, garlic and green pepper; sauté for 10 minutes. Add salt, pepper and tomatoes plus ¼ cup of liquid from the can. Simmer for 20 minutes.

**3**  Remove to electric blender; whirl until there are no big pieces. Add to bowl with chicken and olives; stir thoroughly.

**4**  Fill gun with mixture. Fit with decorator tip.

**5**  Place Toast Cups on baking sheets. Using gun at high speed, pipe mixture into cups. Sprinkle with bacon crumbs.

**6**  Bake in preheated 350-degree oven for 10 minutes, until very hot.

Makes about 4 dozen hors d'oeuvres.

## Chicken Tetrazzinis

Tasty bite-size servings of an old-time favorite.

1½ cups cooked chicken

½ cup egg pastina, cooked

2 tablespoons butter

1 tablespoon all-purpose flour

1 cup chicken broth

2 tablespoons sherry

½ cup heavy cream

2 teaspoons salt

⅛ teaspoon pepper

Pinch of nutmeg

Toast Cups or Pastry Tartlette Shells
(see recipes, pages 43, 44)

¼ cup grated Parmesan cheese

**1** Press chicken through the fine blade of a meat grinder into a bowl. Add pastina and set aside.

**2** Melt butter in a saucepan; blend in flour. Add broth; cook, stirring, over medium heat until slightly thickened. Add sherry and cream; cook, stirring, for another 4 or 5 minutes until heated through.

**3** Add sauce to chicken and pastina. Add salt, pepper and nutmeg. Mix thoroughly.

**4** Fill gun with chicken mixture. Fit with decorator tip.

**5** Place Toast Cups or Pastry Shells on baking sheet. Using gun at high speed, pipe mixture into cups; sprinkle with cheese.

**6** Bake in preheated 350-degree oven for 10 minutes, until very hot.

Makes 5 to 6 dozen hors d'oeuvres.

### Fried Puffs, Flutes and Fingers

*Some of the delicious, exotic tidbits in this section can be fried in advance, then frozen. They are:*

*Chinese Pork and Ginger Fingers*
*Chinese Shrimp Puffs*
*Eggplant Flutes*
*Flounder Fluffs*
*Hot Ham Puffs*
*Reheat while frozen in a 350-degree oven.*

*Turkish Beef Fingers, Mushroom Morsels and Caraway Cauliflower Kisses may also be fried a day or two ahead of time, but should not be frozen. Refrigerate, then reheat shortly before serving.*

*The Beignets Soufflé — a fried puff — is best when prepared and served fresh.*

## Instructions for Making
## Fried Hot Hors d'Oeuvre Puffs

**1**  Cut out rounds of brown paper (from grocery bags, etc.) slightly smaller than the circumference of a deep fryer or 3-quart saucepan.

**2**  Grease each paper on one side with solid shortening.

**3**  Using gun, pipe small mounds (kisses) of puff dough onto greased side of paper, 1 to 1½ inches apart. Each mound should equal about 1½ teaspoons of dough.

**4**  Fill deep fryer or 3-quart saucepan ⅔ full of vegetable oil. Heat to 375 degrees on a deep-fat thermometer.

**5**  Invert the paper into the fryer. The puffs should release themselves in a minute. (If not, remove gently with metal spatula.) Then remove paper and discard. Each paper round should be used only once.

**6**  Fry puffs until golden brown on one side. Turn and brown other side. Remove with a slotted spoon and drain on paper towels or brown paper. Each batch of puffs should take no more than 2 or 3 minutes to fry.

**7**  Remove to baking pan and keep warm in 300-degree oven while frying balance of puffs. Serve hot.

# Pâte
# à Choux

With this basic cream puff dough you can make a variety of dessert pastries, hors d'oeuvre puffs, and shells for main course fillings.

*1  cup water*
*½  cup butter*
*¼  teaspoon salt*
*1  cup sifted all-purpose flour*
*4  large eggs*

**1**  Place water, butter and salt in a saucepan and bring to a boil. Turn off heat; stir in flour all at once. Beat well until mixture forms a mass and leaves sides of pan.

**2**  Cool for 1 minute. Add eggs one at a time, beating well after each addition. Mixture should be smooth and glossy.

**3**  Fill gun with mixture. Fit with decorator tip.

**4**  Use gun at low speed. To make miniature puffs, pipe small mounds of dough onto greased baking sheet about 1 inch apart.

**5**  Bake in preheated 450-degree oven for 15 minutes. Reduce heat to 350 degrees. Bake for another 10 minutes until puffs are nicely browned and have dry, rigid sides. Make a slit in the side of each puff with a small sharp knife. Remove from pan and cool on wire rack.

**6**  Cut a cap off each puff; fill shell with desired hors d'oeuvre filling; replace cap.

Makes about 6 dozen miniature puffs.

## Flounder Fluffs

Lovely and light, these delicately flavored puffs are a combination of fish and cream puff base. A perfect complement to a drink.

2 *cups water*

2 *peppercorns*

2 *teaspoons salt*

2 *tablespoons lemon juice*

1 *pound flounder fillets*

½ *recipe for Pâte à Choux (see page 57)*

   *Dash of cayenne pepper*

   *Vegetable oil for deep frying*

   *Lemon Sauce (recipe follows)*

**1**  In a 10-inch fry pan, boil water, peppercorns, 1 teaspoon salt and 1 tablespoon lemon juice for 5 minutes. Reduce to a simmer. Add fish fillets and cover; poach for 10 minutes. Remove fish to a bowl.

**2**  Using fork or fingers, flake fish very well until there are no chunks. Remove all bones.

**3**  Prepare Pâte à Choux as directed through step 2. Combine with fish, remaining salt, remaining lemon juice and cayenne pepper.

**4**  Fill deep fryer ⅔ full of oil and heat to 375 degrees.

**5**  Fill gun with fish mixture. Fit with decorator tip.

**6**  Use gun at high speed. Follow instructions for making Fried Hot Hors d'Oeuvre Puffs (see page 57).

**7**  Serve with Lemon Sauce for dipping.

Makes about 6 dozen hors d'oeuvres.

### Lemon Sauce

2 *tablespoons grated lemon rind*

¼ *cup lemon juice*

½ *cup mayonnaise*

1 *tablespoon chopped parsley*

1 *tablespoon snipped chives*

1 *teaspoon prepared mustard*

½ *teaspoon salt*

1 *tablespoon horseradish*

1 *clove garlic, finely chopped*

Combine all ingredients in a bowl and mix well.

# Mushroom Morsels

An intriguing delicacy with a dilly of a sauce.

 3 tablespoons butter

½ cup finely chopped onions

½ pound mushrooms, finely chopped

½ recipe for Pâte à Choux (see page 57)

 1 teaspoon salt

⅛ teaspoon pepper

   Vegetable oil for deep frying

   Sour Cream Dill Sauce (recipe follows)

**1** Melt butter in fry pan and sauté onions for 10 minutes. Add mushrooms; cook over medium heat, stirring, for another 5 minutes. Drain mushroom mixture in strainer, pressing out most of the liquid. Place in bowl.

**2** Prepare Pâte à Choux as directed through step 2.

**3** Add mushroom mixture, salt and pepper to Pâte à Choux; stir well.

**4** Fill deep fryer ⅔ full of oil and heat to 375 degrees.

**5** Fill gun with mixture. Fit with decorator tip.

**6** Use gun at high speed. Follow instructions for making Fried Hot Hors d'Oeuvre Puffs (see page 57).

**7** Serve with Sour Cream Dill Sauce for dipping.

Makes 4 to 5 dozen hors d'oeuvres.

## Sour Cream Dill Sauce

½ cup sour cream

¼ cup mayonnaise

 1 tablespoon snipped dill

 1 tablespoon finely chopped scallions

 1 clove garlic, finely chopped

 1 tablespoon horseradish

Combine all ingredients in a bowl and mix well.

## Caraway Cauliflower Kisses

*1  cup cauliflower, cooked*
*½  recipe for Pâte à Choux (see page 57)*
*½  tablespoon caraway seeds*
*1  teaspoon salt*
*Vegetable oil for deep frying*
*Grated Parmesan cheese (optional)*

**1** Mash cauliflower on a plate with a fork. Drain excess water.

**2** Prepare Pâte à Choux as directed through step 2.

**3** In bowl, combine cauliflower, Pâte à Choux, caraway seeds and salt. Mix well.

**4** Fill deep fryer ⅔ full of oil and heat to 375 degrees.

**5** Fill gun with mixture. Fit with decorator tip.

**6** Use gun at high speed. Follow instructions for making Fried Hot Hors d'Oeuvre Puffs (see page 57). If the cauliflower kisses do not detach from the paper by themselves, assist them gently.

**7** Roll in grated cheese, if desired.

Makes 4 to 5 dozen hors d'oeuvres.

## Hot Ham Puffs

*2  tablespoons butter*
*½  cup chopped green pepper*
*½  cup chopped onions*
*¼  pound boiled ham*
*½  recipe for Pâte à Choux (see page 57)*
*½  teaspoon salt*
*Vegetable oil for deep frying*

**1** Melt butter in fry pan; sauté green peppers and onions for 10 minutes. Remove from heat.

**2** Press ham and sautéed peppers and onions through the fine blade of a meat grinder into a bowl.

**3** Prepare Pâte à Choux as directed through step 2.

**4** Add ham mixture and salt to Pâte à Choux; mix well.

**5** Fill deep fryer ⅔ full of oil and heat to 375 degrees.

**6** Fill gun with ham mixture. Fit with decorator tip.

**7** Use gun at high speed. Follow instructions for making Fried Hot Hors d'Oeuvre Puffs (see page 57).

Makes about 4 dozen hors d'oeuvres.

# Chinese
# Shrimp Puffs

Born of the culinary wisdom of the East. It's easy to understand why these little pufflets make such a big hit everywhere.

12-ounce package frozen shelled shrimp, cooked

2  scallions, sliced

8-ounce can water chestnuts, drained

1½  tablespoons soy sauce

2  teaspoons sherry

¼  teaspoon granulated sugar

½  teaspoon salt

¼ -inch slice of fresh ginger root (available in Oriental markets and many gourmet shops)

½  recipe for Pâte à Choux (see page 57)

Vegetable oil for deep frying

Mustard Sauce (recipe follows)

**1**  Press shrimp, scallions and water chestnuts through fine blade of a meat grinder into a bowl. Add soy sauce, sherry, sugar and salt.

**2**  Place ginger root in a garlic press. Squeeze juice into mixture; discard pulp. Mix well.

**3**  Prepare Pâte à Choux as directed through step 2.

**4**  Add shrimp mixture to Pâte à Choux; stir well.

**5**  Fill deep fryer ⅔ full of oil and heat to 375 degrees.

**6**  Fill gun with shrimp mixture. Fit with decorator tip.

**7**  Use gun at high speed. Follow instructions for making Fried Hot Hors d'Oeuvre Puffs (see page 57).

**8**  Serve with Mustard Sauce for dipping.

Makes about 6 dozen hors d'oeuvres.

## Mustard Sauce

¾  cup apricot preserves

¼  cup water

3  tablespoons dry powdered mustard

**1**  Place preserves and water in saucepan over medium low heat. Stir and bring to a boil. Remove from heat and stir in the mustard.

**2**  Cool and place in a small serving bowl.

## Beignets Soufflé

Parmesan cheese adds dash to these melt-in-the-mouth morsels.

¼   cup butter

½   cup water

½   teaspoon salt

½   cup all-purpose flour

¼   cup grated Parmesan cheese

 2  large eggs

     Vegetable oil for deep frying

     Additional grated Parmesan cheese

**1**   Place butter, water and salt in saucepan; cook over medium heat.

**2**   When butter has melted and water is boiling, add flour all at once. Turn off heat. Mix with a wooden spoon until mixture forms a mass and leaves sides of pan.

**3**   Remove from heat. Add cheese and mix well. Add eggs one at a time, mixing well after each addition, until mixture is smooth and glossy.

**4**   Fill deep fryer ⅔ full of oil and heat to 375 degrees.

**5**   Fill gun with mixture. Fit with decorator tip.

**6**   Use gun at high speed. Follow instructions for making Fried Hot Hors d'Oeuvre Puffs (see page 57.) If the Beignets soufflé does not detach from the paper by itself, assist it gently.

**7**   Roll in additional cheese. Serve hot.

Makes about 3 dozen hors d'oeuvres.

## Eggplant Flutes

A traditional combination of ingredients, but unforgettable hors d'oeuvres.

 1  medium eggplant (1 pound)

½   pound ground lamb or beef

 2  tablespoons tomato sauce

1½  tablespoons grated Parmesan cheese

½   teaspoon salt

     Pepper to taste

     Toothpicks

 2  eggs

 4  tablespoons water

⅔   cup packaged bread crumbs

 1  cup vegetable oil

**1**   Peel eggplant; slice in very thin rounds no more than ⅛ inch thick.

**2**   Mix together lamb, tomato sauce, cheese, salt and pepper.

**3**   Fill gun with lamb mixture. Fit with decorator tip.

**4**   Using gun at high speed, press a small amount of mixture onto center of each eggplant round.

**5**   Wrap eggplant around the lamb, holding it together with toothpicks.

**6**   Beat eggs lightly with water. Dip each eggplant flute in eggs, then in bread crumbs.

**7**   Heat oil in 10-inch fry pan. Fry flutes 5 or 6 minutes, turning once or twice. Drain on paper towels. Place on baking sheet and keep warm in oven while frying balance of flutes.

**8**   Remove toothpicks. Serve hot.

Makes 2 to 3 dozen hors d'oeuvres.

## Chinese Pork
## and Ginger Fingers

Bring the subtle flavors of the Orient
to your table.

  1  *pound ground pork*
  4  *scallions, sliced*
     *8-ounce can water chestnuts, drained*
1½  *tablespoons soy sauce*
  1  *teaspoon salt*
  ½ *-inch slice of fresh ginger root (available in Oriental markets and many gourmet shops)*
     *Vegetable oil for deep frying*
     *Soy Dipping Sauce (recipe follows)*

**1**  Press pork, scallions and water chestnuts through the fine blade of a meat grinder into a bowl. Add soy sauce and salt. Blend together with fork or fingers.

**2**  Place ginger root in garlic press. Squeeze juice into mixture; discard pulp. Mix well.

**3**  Cut out 7 or 8 nine-inch rounds of brown paper (from grocery bags, etc.). Grease one side of the paper rounds with solid shortening.

**4**  Fill gun with pork mixture. Fit with decorator tip.

**5**  Using gun at high speed, pipe 9 or 10 three-inch fingers onto each of the greased paper rounds.

**6**  Fill an electric skillet or 10-inch fry pan with 1 inch of oil. Heat to 365 degrees.

**7**  Insert one paper round at a time into the hot oil. The pork fingers should release themselves in a minute. Then remove paper with tongs and discard.

**8**  The pork fingers will take 1 or 2 minutes to cook. Remove with a slotted spoon and drain on paper towels. Place on baking sheet and keep warm in 300-degree oven while frying balance of pork fingers.

**9**  Serve hot with Soy Dipping Sauce.

Makes 4 to 5 dozen hors d'oeuvres.

**Soy Dipping Sauce**

  ½  *cup soy sauce*
  1  *clove garlic, finely chopped*
  2  *teaspoons finely chopped fresh ginger root*
  ½  *teaspoon granulated sugar*
  ½  *teaspoon salt*
  1  *tablespoon sherry*

Combine all ingredients in a bowl and mix well.

## Turkish Beef Fingers

1 pound ground beef
½ cup grated onions
1 cup chopped parsley
1 teaspoon salt
1 large egg
1½ tablespoons curry powder
¼ cup packaged bread crumbs
   Vegetable oil for deep frying
   Curry Sauce (optional; recipe follows)

**1** Place all ingredients except oil and Curry Sauce in a bowl; mix thoroughly.

**2** Cut out 7 or 8 nine-inch rounds of brown paper (from grocery bags, etc.). Grease one side of the paper rounds with solid shortening.

**3** Fill gun with beef mixture. Fit with decorator tip.

**4** Using gun at high speed, pipe 9 or 10 3-inch fingers onto each of the greased paper rounds.

**5** Fill an electric skillet or 10-inch fry pan with 1 inch of oil. Heat to 375 degrees.

**6** Insert one paper round at a time into the hot oil. The beef fingers should release themselves in a minute. Then remove paper with tongs and discard.

**7** The beef fingers will take about 1 minute to cook. Remove with a slotted spoon and drain on paper towels. Place on baking sheet and keep warm in 300-degree oven while frying balance of beef fingers.

**8** Serve hot. Use Curry Sauce for dipping, if desired.

Makes 6 dozen hors d'oeuvres.

### Curry Sauce

2 tablespoons butter
½ cup chopped onions
⅓ cup chopped green pepper
¼ cup flaked coconut
1½ tablespoons all-purpose flour
1 tablespoon curry powder
1 cup chicken broth
½ teaspoon salt

**1** Melt butter in saucepan. Add onions and green pepper; sauté for 10 minutes, stirring occasionally.

**2** Stir in coconut, flour and curry powder. Gradually add broth and salt; stir until hot, smooth and thickened. Remove from heat.

**3** Place mixture in electric blender and whirl until smooth.

*Shown right, Paris-Brest with Chicken and Ham (p. 89), with an individual serving of Orange and Onion Salad (p. 75).*

## Hot Cheese Cookies

*Tasty and unusual, superb with cocktails, these appealing treats are really cheese hors d'oeuvres masquerading as cookies. They make a great snack. You can prepare them quickly and easily with the foodgun in a variety of shapes.*

*Hot cheese cookies may be frozen either before or after baking.*

## Olive Cheese Pastries

Unusual. And unusually good.

*10-ounce jar Spanish pimiento-stuffed olives*

*½ cup butter, softened*

*6 ounces sharp Cheddar cheese, grated*

*1 cup all-purpose flour*

**1** Press olives through the fine blade of a meat grinder into a large bowl. Drain excess liquid very well.

**2** Add remaining ingredients to bowl. Blend thoroughly, using fingers or pastry blender.

**3** Fill gun with mixture. Fit with decorator tip.

**4** Using gun at high speed, pipe small mounds equal to 1½ teaspoons onto ungreased baking sheet, about 1½ inches apart.

**5** Bake in preheated 350-degree oven for about 15 minutes. Serve hot.

Makes 4 to 5 dozen canapés.

*Shown left, Manicotti with Beef (see Manicotti with Ham, p. 83).*

## Three-Cheese
## Cocktail Cookies

Three kinds of cheese merge to make
a new kind of snack.

½  cup butter
½  of an 8-ounce package cream cheese,
      softened
8  ounces sharp Cheddar cheese, grated
1  tablespoon grated Parmesan cheese
1  teaspoon Worcestershire sauce
¼  teaspoon powdered mustard
1  teaspoon salt
1½  cups all-purpose flour

**1**  Place all ingredients in a bowl. Blend
together thoroughly, using fingers or
pastry blender. Then knead mixture in
bowl for a minute or two until blended.

**2**  Fill gun with cheese mixture. Fit with
desired disc.

**3**  Use gun at high speed. Follow instructions for making pressed cookies
(see page 9). Use ungreased baking sheets.

**4**  Bake in preheated 350-degree oven
for 15 minutes. Serve hot.

Makes 5 to 6 dozen canapés.

## Caraway
## Cheese Chews

Who chooses Cheese Chews? Try this
tantalizing tongue-twister (and palate-
pleaser) at your next party.

½  cup butter, softened
8  ounces mellow Cheddar cheese,
      grated
1  tablespoon caraway seeds
1  egg, slightly beaten
¾  teaspoon salt
¾  cup all-purpose flour

**1**  Place all ingredients in a bowl. Blend
together using fingers or pastry blender
until well mixed. If mixture is very soft,
refrigerate for 15 or 20 minutes.

**2**  Fill gun with mixture. Fit with flower
disc.

**3**  Use gun at high speed. Follow instructions for making pressed cookies
(see page 9). Use ungreased baking pan
(jelly roll pan).

**4**  Bake in preheated 400-degree oven
for 15 minutes. Serve hot.

Makes 4 dozen canapés.

## Cheesy Curry 'n Cumin Canapés

Our favorite cookies.

½ cup butter, softened

4 ounces sharp Cheddar cheese, grated

1 teaspoon cumin seeds

1 teaspoon curry powder

½ teaspoon salt

1 cup all-purpose flour

**1** Place all ingredients in a bowl. Blend together using fingers or pastry blender. Knead until well blended.

**2** Fill gun with dough. Fit with flower or heart disc only.

**3** Use gun at high speed. Follow instructions for making pressed cookies (see page 9). Use ungreased baking sheets.

**4** Refrigerate for 1 hour. Bake in preheated 350-degree oven for about 12 minutes until just golden. (Don't worry if they spread a little.) Serve hot.

Makes 4 dozen hors d'oeuvres.

## Blue Strip Teasers

Almond-studded strips of piquant pastry . . . to tease and please the palate.

4-ounce package blue cheese

3-ounce package cream cheese

½ cup butter

¾ cup all-purpose flour

⅛ teaspoon garlic powder

¼ teaspoon salt

¼ cup whole almonds

**1** Using a wooden spoon, press blue cheese through a strainer into a bowl. Add cream cheese, butter, flour, garlic powder and salt.

**2** Grate almonds in electric blender or Mouli grater. Place in strainer; sift into cheese mixture. (Do not use nuts that won't fit through strainer.)

**3** With wooden spoon, mix all ingredients thoroughly.

**4** Fill gun with dough. Fit with saw-toothed disc.

**5** Use gun at high speed. Follow instructions for making cookie fingers (see page 9). Use ungreased baking sheets. Cut dough into 2-inch lengths.

**6** Bake in preheated 350-degree oven for 10 to 12 minutes. Serve hot.

Makes about 4 dozen hors d'oeuvres.

## Puffy Poppy
## Onion Straws

Light, crunchy and delicious. Your guests will grasp at straws like these. Lucky guests!

¾  cup all-purpose flour

½  cup butter, softened

¼  cup sour cream

½  teaspoon salt

2  teaspoons poppy seeds

1  tablespoon dried minced onions

2  tablespoons grated Parmesan cheese

**1**   Place all ingredients in a bowl. Blend together using fingers or pastry blender.

**2**   Fill gun with dough. Fit with decorator tip.

**3**   Use gun at high speed. Moving the gun slowly, pipe out 4 or 5 rows of dough lengthwise onto ungreased baking sheet. Each row should equal the length of the sheet.

**4**   Refrigerate on baking sheet for 1 hour. Bake in preheated 400-degree oven for 10 to 15 minutes. Cut into 3-inch straws. Serve hot.

Makes about 2 dozen hors d'oeuvres.

# Main Courses and Accompaniments

# Main Courses and Accompaniments

Molding and shaping gnocchi . . . stuffing manicotti . . . these were the kinds of dull (and messy) chores that took the pleasure out of cooking. But no more. Just aim the foodgun and the job's done. Neatly.

The plat de resistance calls for equally distinguished accompaniments. Now you can display your virtuosity with vegetables. You'll find that cauliflower, spinach, zucchini, and even the humble potato take to party dressings and play their supporting roles with verve. And you'll enjoy the scintillating things you can do with salads.

Preparing Ahead: The dishes in this section can be prepared a day or two in advance and refrigerated. Stuffed Cauliflower, Gnocchi with Cream Sauce, Spinach and Ricotta Gnocchi, and Baked Zucchini Boats can be prepared ahead but should not be baked until the day they're served.

You can freeze the following:
Basic Tomato Sauce
Manicotti with Ham
Olive Cheese Puffle
Stuffed Rigatoni
Triple Cheese 'n Spinach Pie

# Gazpacho
# Mold

This summery dish—with all the zesty flavors of sunny Spain—can brighten your table all year 'round.

1  cup fresh peeled, diced tomatoes

1  cup diced green pepper

1  cup diced celery

1  cup diced cucumber

¼  cup sliced scallions

1  tablespoon fresh snipped chives

1  tablespoon fresh chopped parsley

1  clove garlic, finely chopped

¼  cup wine vinegar

¼  cup vegetable oil

1  teaspoon salt

⅛  teaspoon freshly ground pepper

1  teaspoon Worcestershire sauce

2  envelopes unflavored gelatin

2  cups tomato juice

½  cup sour cream

1    Combine first 8 ingredients in a bowl and mix. Remove 1 cup of mixture to electric blender container.

2    Combine vinegar, oil, salt, pepper and Worcestershire sauce; mix well. Pour over vegetables in bowl and toss the salad, mixing thoroughly.

3    Sprinkle gelatin over ½ cup of the tomato juice to soften. Stir over hot water to dissolve. Add gelatin juice plus another ½ cup of tomato juice to mixture in blender; whirl until smooth. Place in bowl with vegetables. Add remaining tomato juice; mix thoroughly.

4    Spoon mixture into oiled 6-cup ring mold and refrigerate overnight. Unmold on a bed of lettuce on a serving platter.

5    Fill gun with sour cream. Fit with decorator tip.

6    Using gun at high speed, pipe swirls of sour cream on top of ring.

8 to 12 salad or first course servings.

## Scandinavian Veal and Herring Salad

Velvety veal and sturdy herring are key factors in this harmonious arrangement of Nordic niceties.

9-ounce jar herring in wine sauce
1½ cups leftover cold cooked veal
2 8-ounce cans diced beets, drained
2 cups diced boiled potatoes
  (2 medium-size potatoes)
½ cup chopped onions
½ cup peeled, cored and diced apple
¼ cup finely chopped dill pickles
1 tablespoon fresh snipped dill
1¼ cups sour cream
¼ cup wine vinegar
2 teaspoons prepared mustard
¼ cup vegetable oil
Salt
Freshly ground pepper
2 hard-cooked eggs

**1**   Drain herring, discarding onions in jar. Dice into ½-inch pieces.

**2**   Dice veal into ½-inch pieces.

**3**   Reserve 2 tablespoons of the beets. In a large bowl, combine the remaining beets, herring, veal, potatoes, onions, apple, pickles and dill.

**4**   Mix together ¼ cup of the sour cream, vinegar, mustard, oil and salt and pepper to taste. Combine with ingredients in bowl; toss gently but thoroughly.

**5**   Pack salad into a 6-cup mold or bowl. Refrigerate. When cold, unmold on serving platter.

**6**   Chop eggs and sprinkle over top of salad.

**7**   Press reserved beets through a strainer into a bowl. Add remaining cup of sour cream; mix well.

**8**   Fill gun with sour cream beet mixture. Fit with decorator tip.

**9**   Using gun at high speed, pipe rosettes around bottom of salad mold.

6 servings.

———

*Variation:* Chicken or pork may be substituted for the veal.

# Orange and Onion Salad

A lovely idea . . . rounds of fresh juicy orange and red onion, with a dressing of fruit and cream.

8 navel oranges

1 cup thinly sliced red onions

2½ tablespoons lemon juice

½ cup vegetable oil

¼ teaspoon fresh black pepper

¾ teaspoon salt

Pinch of sugar

Citrus Dressing (recipe follows)

**1**  Grate rind of 1 or 2 oranges to get 1½ tablespoons grated rind. Reserve for Citrus Dressing.

**2**  Remove peel and white underskin from all the oranges. Cut into ¼-inch rounds. Place in bowl with sliced onions.

**3**  Combine lemon juice, oil and seasonings; stir well. Pour over oranges and onions; toss to blend.

**4**  Divide salad evenly among 8 stem glasses (9-ounce size at least).

**5**  Fill gun with Citrus Dressing. Fit with decorator tip.

**6**  Using gun at high speed, pipe dressing in decorative swirls over each salad serving. Refrigerate.

8 individual servings.

## Citrus Dressing

1 large lemon

1 large egg, beaten

½ cup granulated sugar

1½ tablespoons grated orange rind (reserved from preceding recipe)

1 cup heavy cream

**1**  Grate rind of lemon to get 1 tablespoon grated rind. Squeeze lemon to get 2 tablespoons lemon juice.

**2**  Combine lemon rind, lemon juice, egg, sugar and orange rind in a saucepan. Cook, stirring, over low heat for about 5 minutes, until thick. Cool.

**3**  Whip heavy cream until stiff. Combine gently with cool sauce.

## Chicken Stuffed Avocado

2  cups cooked chicken, cut into ½ -inch
      cubes
½  cup coarsely chopped almonds
¾  cup chopped celery
½  cup canned water chestnuts, sliced
      and drained
½  teaspoon salt
     Pepper to taste
½  cup mayonnaise
3  ripe avocados
     Avocado Dressing (recipe follows)

**1**   Place chicken in bowl with almonds,
celery, water chestnuts, salt, pepper and
mayonnaise. Mix well and taste for
seasonings.

**2**   Cut avocados in half lengthwise and
remove pits. Cut off thin slice from bottom
of each avocado half so it will stand upright. Fill the halves with chicken salad.
Place on a bed of lettuce on a serving
platter.

**3**   Fill gun with Avocado Dressing. Fit
with decorator tip.

**4**   Using gun at low speed, pipe decorative swirl of dressing over each stuffed
avocado.

6 luncheon servings.

### Avocado Dressing

1  ripe avocado
⅛  teaspoon garlic powder
¼  teaspoon salt
⅛  teaspoon cayenne pepper
1  tablespoon canned tacos sauce
½  cup heavy cream

**1**   Peel and pit the avocado; mash it in a
bowl, using a fork. Stir in garlic, salt,
pepper and tacos sauce.

**2**   Whip heavy cream until stiff. Fold into
avocado mixture.

———

*Note:* Leftover tacos sauce can be stored
in refrigerator. Heat and serve with ham-
burgers.

*Suggestion:* Save a pit for planting. To
start your avocado tree, rinse the pit in
warm water and pat dry. About ⅓ of the
way up from the dimpled bottom, push
four toothpicks into the pit at equidistant
intervals to allow you to suspend it from
the top of a glass. Fill the glass with tepid
water until it covers about ½ inch of the
pit. Keep the pit in a warm place and it
will begin to take root.

## Ratatouille Tart

Pretty as a garden and just as enticing.

½ *recipe for Short Pastry (see page 118)*
3 *tablespoons vegetable oil*
1 *cup chopped onions*
1 *cup chopped celery*
½ *cup chopped green pepper*
1 *large clove garlic, chopped*
1 *teaspoon salt*
28-ounce *can Italian style tomatoes, diced*
1 *or 2 small zucchini*
2 *or 3 thick scallions*
3 *or 4 mushroom caps*
  *Grated Parmesan cheese*
  *Packaged bread crumbs*
1 *tablespoon butter*
½ *cup ricotta cheese*

**1**  Prepare Short Pastry as directed. Line a 9-inch pie plate with dough. Follow directions for "Making a Pie Shell" through step 4. Set aside.

**2**  Heat oil in fry pan. Add onions, celery and green pepper; sauté for 10 minutes. Add garlic, salt and tomatoes with liquid from the can. Simmer over medium low heat for 30 minutes, until thickened. Remove from heat and cool.

**3**  Pour cooled tomato mixture into pastry shell.

**4**  Slice zucchini into ¼-inch rounds and place in overlapping slices around the outer edge of the tart, on top of tomato mixture.

**5**  Slice scallions into ⅛-inch rounds, using only the whites of the scallions. Make 2 circles of scallions inside the zucchini slices.

**6**  Save one whole mushroom cap. Slice others ⅛-inch thick. Arrange mushroom slices in overlapping pattern in remaining space. Place whole mushroom cap in center, stem side down.

**7**  Sprinkle top with Parmesan and bread crumbs. Dot with butter.

**8**  Bake in preheated 400-degree oven for 30 minutes. Cool on wire rack.

**9**  Fill gun with ricotta. Fit with decorator tip.

**10**  Using gun at high speed, pipe a circle of ricotta on top of scallions. Pipe another circle of ricotta around the center mushroom. Serve warm or cold.

6 to 12 appetizer or side dish servings.

## Empañada Pie

Bravo! We should thank our Chilean friends for this delectable dish.

½ recipe for Short Pastry (see page 118)

⅓ cup chopped onions

⅓ cup chopped green pepper

2 tablespoons vegetable oil

1 pound raw ground beef

½ cup canned diced pears

½ cup canned diced peaches

1½ tablespoons snipped chives

1 cup fresh peeled and diced tomatoes

¾ cup dark seedless raisins

½ teaspoon cinnamon

½ teaspoon salt

2 tablespoons sherry

1 large egg

¾ cup sharp Cheddar cheese (crock type)

**1** Prepare Short Pastry as directed. Line a 9-inch pie plate with the dough, following directions for "Making a Pie Shell" through step 4. Set aside.

**2** Sauté onions and green pepper in oil for 10 minutes. Remove from heat; set aside.

**3** Place all other ingredients in a bowl, except Cheddar cheese. Mix thoroughly. Add sautéed onions and green pepper; mix again.

**4** Spoon into pastry-lined pie plate and cover with aluminum foil. Place pie on baking pan to catch spills.

**5** Bake in preheated 375-degree oven for 40 minutes. Uncover and bake another 10 to 15 minutes.

**6** Remove from oven and pour off liquid that has accumulated around edges. (Don't worry if meat has shrunk from sides of pastry.) Cool on wire rack for 20 minutes.

**7** Fill gun with Cheddar cheese that has been out of refrigerator for 30 minutes. Fit with decorator tip.

**8** Using gun at high speed, cover pie with lattice topping, piping 5 rows of cheese across and five rows down. Serve warm.

6 servings.

# Coquilles Saint-Jacques

1 cup dry white wine

½ cup water

½ teaspoon dried thyme

½ bay leaf

1 small onion

Sprig of parsley

2 peppercorns

1 pound bay scallops (cut into halves) or sea scallops (cut into quarters)

½ pound mushrooms, sliced

White Wine Sauce (recipe follows)

6 buttered scallop shells

½ cup grated Swiss cheese

2 tablespoons butter

Duchesse Potatoes (recipe follows)

1   Simmer the wine, water, thyme, bay leaf, onion, parsley and peppercorns in a saucepan for 5 minutes. Add scallops and mushrooms. If necessary, add water to just cover ingredients. Bring quickly to a simmer and cover. Continue simmering scallops exactly 2 minutes.

2   Using a slotted spoon, quickly remove scallops and mushrooms to a bowl. Reserve liquid in saucepan for use in White Wine Sauce.

3   Combine White Wine Sauce with scallops and mushrooms.

4   Spoon mixture into scallop shells. Sprinkle with cheese and dot with butter.

5   Fill gun with Duchesse Potatoes. Fit with decorator tip.

6   Using gun at high speed, pipe a decorative border of potatoes around the inside edge of the scallop shells.

7   Place under broiler for about 5 minutes, until cheese is browned.

6 servings.

————

Variation: Coquilles Saint-Jacques may be placed in a casserole instead of scallop shells. Pipe potatoes around inside edge of casserole; broil for about 5 minutes. Spoon cooked peas inside the ring of potatoes.

Recipes for White Wine Sauce and Duchesse Potatoes appear on next page.

## White Wine Sauce

3 tablespoons butter

¼ cup all-purpose flour

1½ cups reserved hot scallop liquid, strained

2 egg yolks

¾ cup heavy cream

Salt and pepper to taste

**1**  Melt butter in saucepan. Stir in flour and hot scallop liquid. Continue stirring until thickened and smooth.

**2**  Mix together the egg yolks and heavy cream. While stirring with a wire whisk, gradually add hot scallop sauce to yolk mixture.

**3**  Transfer sauce back into pan; add salt and pepper. Continue stirring and bring to a boil. Remove from heat. Combine with scallops and mushrooms as directed.

## Duchesse Potatoes

3 medium potatoes, peeled and halved

1½ tablespoons butter

Salt and pepper to taste

1 whole egg

1 egg yolk

**1**  Cook potatoes in boiling salted water to cover, until tender but firm. Drain well.

**2**  Mash potatoes until there are no lumps.

**3**  Add butter, salt and pepper. Beat with wooden spoon.

**4**  Lightly beat whole egg and yolk together. Add to potato mixture; beat until fluffy. Fill gun with potatoes as directed.

# Triple Cheese 'n Spinach Pie

9-inch unbaked Pastry Shell (see recipe, page 118)

2 tablespoons butter

1 cup chopped onions

3 large eggs

15-ounce container ricotta cheese

1 cup sour cream

½ cup grated mozzarella cheese

¼ cup grated Parmesan cheese

10-ounce package frozen chopped spinach, cooked and very well drained

Salt and pepper to taste

**1**  Prepare Pastry Shell as directed.

**2**  Melt butter in fry pan. Add onions; sauté for 10 minutes. Remove from heat.

**3**  In a large bowl, beat eggs. Add 1 cup of ricotta, sour cream, mozzarella, Parmesan, spinach, salt, pepper and sautéed onions. Mix well with a wooden spoon; taste for seasonings. Pour into Pastry Shell.

**4**  Bake in preheated 350-degree oven for 45 minutes, until a sharp knife inserted in center comes out clean. Place on a wire rack.

**5**  Fill gun with remaining ricotta. Fit with decorator tip.

**6**  Using gun at low speed, pipe on a lattice topping, an S-shaped design around the rim, or decorative swirls over the surface. Serve hot.

6 to 8 luncheon or first course servings.

## Olive Cheese Puffle

A novel way to serve bread and cheese and olives. Bake 'em together in a deviled custard that's devilishly good.

> 6 *slices white bread*
>
> *Butter*
>
> 16 *Spanish green pimiento-stuffed olives, sliced*
>
> 1½ *cups grated sharp Cheddar cheese*
>
> 5 *large eggs*
>
> 1 *teaspoon dry powdered mustard*
>
> ½ *teaspoon salt*
>
> 1 *teaspoon Worcestershire sauce*
>
> 2½ *cups milk*
>
> ⅓ *recipe Olive Cheese Pastry (see page 67)*

**1**  Remove crusts from bread; butter one side of each slice.

**2**  Place alternating layers of bread, olives and cheese in a greased 1½-quart baking dish.

**3**  In a bowl, beat eggs with mustard, salt and Worcestershire sauce. Add milk; mix well.

**4**  Pour egg mixture over bread, olive and cheese layers. Cover and leave at room temperature for 2 hours.

**5**  Set covered baking dish in a larger pan half-filled with boiling water. Bake in preheated 350-degree oven for 45 minutes. Remove from oven.

**6**  Prepare ⅓ recipe for Olive Cheese Pastry as directed through step 2.

**7**  Fill gun with Olive Cheese Pastry mixture. Fit with decorator tip.

**8**  Using gun at high speed, pipe small mounds over surface of cheese puffle. Put in oven uncovered and bake another 15 minutes. (Do not replace in pan with water.)

4 to 6 main course luncheon or dinner servings.

## Spinach and Ricotta Gnocchi

These dumplings will win huzzahs.

2  *tablespoons butter*

2  *tablespoons grated onion*

10-ounce *package frozen chopped spinach, thawed and very well drained*

¾  *cup ricotta cheese*

⅔  *cup all-purpose flour*

2  *egg yolks*

⅛  *teaspoon ground nutmeg*

1½  *teaspoons salt*

1  *cup grated Parmesan cheese*

2  *cups Basic Tomato Sauce (recipe appears on next page)*

*Additional grated Parmesan cheese*

**1**  Heat butter in fry pan. Add onion; sauté for 2 minutes. Add spinach; sauté over medium heat for 5 minutes, stirring often.

**2**  Place spinach and onion in a bowl. Add ricotta and flour; mix with a wooden spoon. Add egg yolks, nutmeg, salt and Parmesan; mix thoroughly.

**3**  Grease a shallow casserole. Set aside.

**4**  Bring 4 quarts of lightly salted water to a boil. Continue boiling gently.

**5**  Fill gun with spinach mixture. Fit with decorator tip.

**6**  Use gun at high speed. Hold gun over the lightly boiling water; pipe dough out gently. As it comes through, cut off ½ - to ¾-inch lengths with a pair of scissors, letting dough drop into the water. Cook half the dough this way for 2 to 3 minutes after water returns to a boil. (You may have to raise the heat for a minute.) Remove gnocchi with a slotted spoon; place in the casserole. Repeat the process using the balance of the dough.

**7**  Cover gnocchi with Basic Tomato Sauce; sprinkle with additional Parmesan. Bake in preheated 350-degree oven for 15 to 20 minutes.

4 to 6 luncheon or side dish servings.

———

*Variation:* Gnocchi may be served with butter and cheese instead of tomato sauce. Drizzle 4 tablespoons of melted butter over gnocchi; sprinkle with grated Parmesan. Bake in preheated 350-degree oven for 10 to 15 minutes.

## Basic Tomato Sauce

- 3 tablespoons olive oil
- 1 cup chopped onions
- ½ cup chopped celery
- 1 carrot, grated
- 35-ounce can peeled Italian tomatoes, with liquid
- 6-ounce can tomato paste
- 1 bay leaf
- ¼ teaspoon granulated sugar
- 1 teaspoon salt
- ⅛ teaspoon pepper
- ¼ teaspoon oregano

**1**   Heat oil in large fry pan. Sauté onions, celery and carrot for 10 minutes.

**2**   Add tomatoes and can liquid. Cut up the tomatoes in the pan. Add tomato paste, bay leaf, sugar, salt and pepper.

**3**   Simmer, uncovered, for 2 hours. Add oregano; cook for 5 minutes more.

**4**   Purée sauce through a food mill.

Makes about 5 cups of sauce.

# Manicotti with Ham

- 12 manicotti noodles
- 1 pound cooked ham
- ⅔ cup grated Swiss cheese
- ⅔ cup grated mozzarella cheese
- ½ cup heavy cream
- 2 large eggs, beaten
- 2 tablespoons packaged bread crumbs
  Salt and pepper
  Cream Sauce (see recipe, page 85)
  Grated Parmesan cheese

**1**   Cook manicotti according to package directions. Drain; set aside.

**2**   Press ham through fine blade of a meat grinder into a large bowl. Add Swiss and mozzarella cheeses, heavy cream, eggs, bread crumbs, and salt and pepper to taste. Mix well.

**3**   Fill gun with ham mixture. Fit with decorator tip.

**4**   Using gun at high speed, pipe mixture into both ends of manicotti.

**5**   Grease a large, shallow casserole. Spoon a small amount of Cream Sauce over bottom. Place manicotti in casserole. Cover with remaining Cream Sauce; sprinkle with Parmesan.

**6**   Bake in preheated 350-degree oven for 25 minutes, until very hot.

6 servings.

*Variation:* Manicotti may be filled with chicken and spinach, beef or cheese.

# Stuffed Rigatoni

Pasta with a savory filling of spinach and meat.

8  ounces rigatoni noodles (about 50)

1  cup cooked chicken

10-ounce package frozen chopped spinach, cooked and very well drained

1  large egg, beaten

¼  cup heavy cream

¼  cup grated Parmesan cheese

1  tablespoon chopped parsley

1  clove garlic, finely chopped

½  teaspoon salt

⅛  teaspoon pepper

¼  teaspoon nutmeg

2  cups Basic Tomato Sauce (see recipe, page 83); or 16-ounce jar spaghetti sauce

Additional grated Parmesan cheese

**1**  Cook rigatoni according to package directions. Do not overcook. Drain; set aside.

**2**  Press chicken through the fine blade of a meat grinder into a bowl. Add spinach, egg, cream, cheese, parsley, garlic, salt, pepper and nutmeg. Mix together thoroughly; taste for seasoning.

**4**  Fill gun with mixture. Fit with decorator tip.

**5**  Stand rigatoni vertically and pipe mixture into them, using high speed.

**6**  Grease a shallow casserole. Spoon a small amount of Basic Tomato Sauce over bottom. Place rigatoni on top of sauce; sprinkle with Parmesan.

**7**  Bake in preheated 350-degree oven for 25 minutes, until very hot.

Makes 6 to 8 main course or first course servings.

———

Variation: Rigatoni may be stuffed with ham and cheese mixture or beef.

## Gnocchi
## with Cream Sauce

More dumplings, Italian style.

½  cup plus 2 tablespoons butter
1  cup water
1  teaspoon salt
   Pinch of nutmeg
1  cup all-purpose flour
4  large eggs
   Cream Sauce (recipe follows)
   Grated Parmesan cheese

**1**   Place ½ cup butter, water, salt and nutmeg in a saucepan. Bring to a boil; add flour all at once. Turn off heat. Stir quickly with a wooden spoon until mixture forms a mass and leaves sides of pan. Remove from heat.

**2**   Add eggs one at a time, beating well after each addition until mixture is smooth and glossy.

**3**   Bring 5 quarts of lightly salted water to a boil. Continue simmering.

**4**   Fill gun with paste. Fit with decorator tip.

**5**   Use gun at high speed. Hold gun over the *barely* simmering water; pipe paste out gently. As it comes through, cut off 1-inch lengths with a pair of scissors, letting paste drop into the water. Poach half the paste this way for 3 or 4 minutes. Remove with a slotted spoon; place gently in a colander to drain. Repeat the process using the balance of the paste.

**6**   Grease a shallow casserole. Spoon a thin layer of Cream Sauce over bottom. Add half the gnocchi; cover with half the Cream Sauce; sprinkle with Parmesan. Place remaining gnocchi on top; cover with remaining Cream Sauce and Parmesan. Dot with 2 tablespoons butter.

**7**   Bake in preheated 350-degree oven for about 25 minutes.

4 to 6 luncheon or side dish servings.

### Cream Sauce

6  tablespoons butter
6  tablespoons all-purpose flour
2  cups milk
½  cup heavy cream
1  teaspoon salt
   Pepper to taste

Melt butter in saucepan. Add flour; stir with a wire whisk. Add milk gradually; cook, stirring vigorously until mixture is hot, smooth and thickened. Add heavy cream, salt and pepper. Taste for seasonings. Remove from heat.

# Meatloaf
# with Potatoes

People who used to complain, "What, meatloaf *again!*" are going to eat their words—and relish every mouthful.

  2  *large eggs*
  1  *cup milk*
  3  *slices white bread, diced*
  2  *pounds ground beef*
  1/3  *cup finely minced onions*
1 1/2  *teaspoons salt*
  1/8  *teaspoon pepper*
  *16-ounce can whole peeled tomatoes*
  1/2  *cup sliced onions*
     *Duchesse Potato Rings (see recipe, page 93)*
     *Paprika*

**1**  In a large bowl, beat eggs lightly with milk. Add bread; let it soak for 5 minutes to soften. Mix well; mash with a fork.

**2**  Add beef, minced onions, salt and pepper. Mix well.

**3**  Place mixture in an 8 x 12 x 2-inch baking pan. Shape into a loaf approximately 4 x 10 x 4 inches. Fill spaces between meat loaf and sides of pan with tomatoes and sliced onions. Pour juice from tomato can over meat. Bake in a preheated 350-degree oven for 1 1/2 hours.

**4**  Prepare Duchesse Potatoes as directed through step 3.

**5**  Remove meatloaf from oven; place in an oven-to-table baking dish. Reserve tomato onion mixture in baking pan.

**6**  Fill gun with potato mixture. Fit with decorator tip.

**7**  Using gun at high speed, pipe an S-shaped decoration lengthwise down the middle of the meatloaf. Pipe a decorative border around bottom edge of loaf. Dust potatoes with paprika.

**8**  Return meatloaf to preheated 400-degree oven for 10 minutes, until potatoes are lightly browned and hot.

**9**  On top of range, heat tomato onion mixture in the baking pan. Remove excess fat with a spoon.

**10**  Press hot tomato onion mixture through a food mill into a gravy boat. Serve with meatloaf.

6 servings.

# Bread Cake
# with Beef and Eggplant

Take a crusty loaf of Italian bread, stuff it with mushrooms and beef in a superbly seasoned tomato sauce . . . and you've come up with a winning combination.

  6  tablespoons vegetable oil

  2  cups finely chopped onions

  ½  pound mushrooms, sliced

  2  pounds ground beef

  ¼  cup grated Parmesan cheese

1½  cups tomato sauce

  1-pound eggplant, peeled and diced

  1  tablespoon butter

  1  tablespoon all-purpose flour

  2  tablespoons heavy cream

     Salt and pepper to taste

  1  pound round loaf of Italian bread,
        unsliced

     Additional grated Parmesan cheese

     Additional butter

**1**  Heat 4 tablespoons oil in large fry pan. Add onions; sauté for 15 minutes until soft. Remove about ⅓ of the onions from the pan and set them aside.

**2**  Add mushrooms to the pan; cook over medium heat for 5 minutes. Drain liquid; place mixture in bowl.

**3**  Heat 2 tablespoons oil in the fry pan. Break up meat in the pan and cook over medium heat, stirring often, until thoroughly browned. Drain oil. Add cheese and tomato sauce. Mix well; simmer for 5 minutes. Remove from heat and add mushroom mixture. Set aside.

**4**  Cook eggplant in boiling salted water to cover until soft; drain well. Mash with a fork. Place in strainer and press out water with a wooden spoon.

**5**  Heat reserved onions in a saucepan with 1 tablespoon butter. Add flour and stir. Gradually add heavy cream; stir until thick. Add eggplant, salt and pepper. Remove from heat.

**6**  Cut bread in half horizontally. Remove some of the soft insides from both the top and bottom halves.

**7**  Place bottom of bread in an oven-to-table serving dish and fill with meat mixture, piling it high. Cover with top of bread, pressing down on meat.

**8**  Fill gun with eggplant mixture. Fit with decorator tip.

**9**  Using gun at high speed, pipe eggplant over top of bread in decorative swirls. Sprinkle with additional Parmesan and dot with butter.

**10**  Cover carefully with aluminum foil and bake in preheated 350-degree oven for 30 minutes. Place a pan of water on bottom of oven during baking to prevent bread from drying out. After 30 minutes, remove foil from eggplant; bake 10 minutes more uncovered.

8 servings.

# Fish and Spinach Pâté

1   tablespoon butter

½   cup chopped onions

2   pounds flounder fillets

¼   cup heavy cream

3   large eggs

1   teaspoon salt

⅛   teaspoon white pepper

1   cup butter, softened

½   of a 10-ounce package frozen chopped spinach, cooked and very well drained

2   hard-cooked eggs, sliced

Tangy Sauce for Fish (recipe appears on next page)

**1**   Melt tablespoon of butter in fry pan. Add onions; sauté until tender. Remove from heat and set aside.

**2**   Cut away the row of small bones down the middle of each fillet. Reserve half the fillets. Cut remainder into 1-inch pieces.

**3**   In three batches, purée the small pieces in a blender with the cream, eggs, salt and pepper, adding butter to the last batch. Remove to a bowl.

**4**   Fold ¼ cup of the spinach into the fish purée.

**5**   Combine remaining spinach with the sautéed onions.

**6**   Grease a 9 x 5 x 3-inch loaf pan. Spoon half the fish mixture into pan; cover with half the reserved flounder fillets. (Don't let fillets touch sides of pan.) Place spinach onion mixture on top; cover with egg slices; top with remaining flounder fillets. Spoon remaining fish mixture over all and spread evenly.

**7**   Cover pan with buttered waxed paper, then a sheet of aluminum foil.

**8**   Set in larger pan. Pour enough boiling water in outer pan to reach halfway up the sides of loaf pan.

**9**   Bake in preheated 300-degree oven for 55 minutes. Remove loaf pan from the water and cool. Refrigerate overnight.

**10**   With a sharp knife, release the pâté from the sides of the pan. Dip the pan in hot water and invert the pâté onto a serving platter.

**11**   Fill gun with Tangy Sauce. Fit with decorator tip.

**12**   Using gun at high speed, pipe decorative border around top and bottom of pâté. Any remaining sauce may be piped around edge of platter.

10 to 12 appetizer servings or 6 to 8 luncheon servings.

## Tangy Sauce for Fish

   3  tablespoons ketchup

   1  tablespoon cold water

   1  envelope unflavored gelatin

  1/3  cup sour cream

  1/2  cup mayonnaise

   2  tablespoons finely chopped parsley

   1  tablespoon finely snipped chives

   1  tablespoon horseradish

  1/4  cup heavy cream

**1**  Combine ketchup with water. Sprinkle gelatin over mixture to soften. Stir over hot water to dissolve. Set aside to cool.

**2**  Mix sour cream and mayonnaise. Add parsley, chives, horseradish and cooled gelatin mixture. Mix thoroughly.

**3**  Beat heavy cream until stiff. Fold into sauce.

**4**  Chill until it just sets.

## Paris-Brest with Chicken and Ham

   7  tablespoons butter

   5  shallots, chopped

  1/2  pound mushrooms, sliced

   6  tablespoons all-purpose flour

  1 1/4  cups chicken broth

  1/3  cup heavy cream

   1  tablespoon sherry

  1/2  teaspoon salt

  1/8  teaspoon pepper

   2  cups cooked chicken, cut in large cubes

   1  cup cooked ham, cut in large cubes
      Paris-Brest (see recipe, page 128)

**1**  Melt 3 tablespoons butter in fry pan. Add shallots; sauté for 2 minutes. Add mushrooms; cook, stirring occasionally, for 5 minutes. Set aside.

**2**  Melt remaining 4 tablespoons butter in saucepan. Add flour and stir. Gradually add broth, stirring rapidly with wire whisk until thick and smooth. Add heavy cream, sherry, salt and pepper. Cook, stirring, until sauce comes to a boil. Reduce heat and cook, stirring constantly, for another 5 minutes. Remove from heat.

**3**  Add mushroom mixture, chicken and ham; stir. Set aside.

**4**  Prepare Paris-Brest as directed, through step 4. Cut it in half horizontally. Place bottom half in lightly greased oven-to-table serving dish. Fill with chicken and ham mixture. Cover with top half of pastry.

**5**  Bake in preheated 350-degree oven for 25 to 30 minutes, until very hot.

6 to 8 servings.

# Chicken Breast Florentine

Tender chicken breasts, bordered with fluffed potatoes, scattered with sautéed mushrooms. And beneath it all—a buttered bed of lemon-spiked spinach.

>   *Duchesse Potato Rings (see recipe, page 93)*
> 3  *10-ounce packages frozen spinach*
> 1  *tablespoon lemon juice*
> ¼  *cup grated Parmesan cheese*
> ½  *cup plus 2 tablespoons butter*
> 4  *whole chicken breasts, skinned, boned and halved.*
>    *Flour for dredging*
> 1  *teaspoon salt*
>    *Paprika*
> 1  *pound mushrooms, sliced*

**1**   Prepare Duchesse Potatoes as directed through step 3. Set aside.

**2**   Cook spinach according to package directions. Squeeze out excess water. Spread spinach evenly over bottom of greased oven-to-table baking dish that measures about 9 x 13 x 2 inches. Sprinkle spinach with lemon juice and Parmesan. Dot with 1 tablespoon butter.

**3**   Dredge chicken in flour. Melt 6 tablespoons butter in large fry pan; add chicken, cook over medium low heat for about 8 minutes on each side. Place chicken on top of the spinach bed; sprinkle with salt.

**4**   Fill gun with Duchesse Potatoes. Fit with decorator tip.

**5**   Using gun at high speed, pipe a border of potatoes around the edge of the baking dish. Dust with paprika.

**6**   Bake in preheated 425-degree oven for 10 to 15 minutes, until potatoes are lightly browned and hot.

**7**   Heat remaining 3 tablespoons of butter in fry pan. Add mushrooms; sauté for about 10 minutes, stirring often, until tender.

**8**   After baking dish is out of oven, spoon hot mushrooms over center.

8 servings.

# Baked
# Zucchini Boats

Set sail with these tasty stuffed vegetables. A good traveling companion for roast meat or chicken.

6  *6-inch zucchini*
6  *tablespoons butter*
¾  *cup finely chopped onions*
1  *tablespoon all-pupose flour*
⅓  *cup heavy cream*
¼  *cup packaged bread crumbs*
4  *tablespoons grated Parmesan cheese*
   *Salt and pepper to taste*

**1**    Trim stem ends of zucchini. Slice off a third lengthwise, leaving a canoe-like bottom.

**2**    Place top and bottom sections of zucchini in boiling salted water to cover; cook for 5 minutes. Drain in colander and run under cold water to permit handling.

**3**    Scoop out the pulp from the top and bottom sections, being careful not to tear bottom shells. Discard top shells. Chop the pulp and squeeze out as much moisture as possible. Dry bottom shells with paper towels.

**4**    Melt 4 tablespoons of butter in a fry pan. Add onions; sauté for 10 minutes, until very soft. Add the zucchini pulp; cook for 5 minutes until very tender. Mash mixture in the pan with a fork.

**5**    Sprinkle mixture with flour; stir. Add heavy cream and cook for 2 minutes. Add bread crumbs, 2 tablespoons of Parmesan, salt and pepper. Mix thoroughly and remove from heat.

**6**    Fill gun with zucchini mixture. Fit with decorator tip.

**7**    Using gun at high speed, pipe mixture into dry zucchini shells. Sprinkle with remaining Parmesan and dot with remaining butter.

**8**    Place zucchini boats in greased shallow casserole or au gratin dish. Bake in preheated 400-degree oven for 20 minutes, until very hot.

6 servings.

———

*Variation:* Baked zucchini boats may also be stuffed with meat. Prepare recipe as directed through step 5. Add ⅓ pound ground beef to mixture and mix well. Follow steps 6 through 8.

## Duchesse Tomatoes

6  *medium tomatoes*
   *Salt and pepper*
½  *recipe for Duchesse Potato Rings, omitting paprika (see page 93)*
1  *tablespoon melted butter*
¼  *cup grated Parmesan cheese*

**1**  Cut a slice off the stem end of each tomato and discard. Scoop out the centers and sprinkle the cavities lightly with salt and pepper. Place tomato shells in a greased baking dish.

**2**  Prepare Duchesse Potato Rings as directed through step 3.

**3**  Fill gun with potato mixture. Fit with decorator tip.

**4**  Using gun at high speed, pipe potatoes into tomato shells, swirling and mounding them high.

**5**  Brush potatoes with melted butter. Sprinkle with Parmesan.

**6**  Bake in preheated 450-degree oven for about 15 minutes, until browned and hot.

6 servings.

———

*Note:* Tomato pulp may be stored in refrigerator and used for making tomato sauce.

## Sausage Potatoes

6  *large baking potatoes, scrubbed and dried*
6  *breakfast sausages*
3  *tablespoons butter*
½  *cup sour cream*
   *Salt and pepper to taste*
   *Paprika*

**1**  Bake potatoes in preheated 425-degree oven for 45 to 60 minutes, until soft.

**2**  Cook sausages according to package directions; cut each into 8 slices. Set aside.

**3**  Cut a slice off the top of each potato. Scoop out insides into a bowl, being careful not to break the shells. Place shells on baking pan; set aside.

**4**  Add butter to the scooped potatoes; mash together well. Beat in sour cream; add salt and pepper.

**5**  Fill gun with potato mixture. Fit with decorator tip.

**6**  Using gun at high speed, pipe potatoes into the reserved shells, filling each half full; cover each with sausage slices; top with balance of potatoes. Sprinkle lightly with paprika.

**7**  Return to preheated 425-degree oven and bake for about 15 minutes, until browned and hot.

6 servings.

## Blue Cheese Potatoes

Your stock is sure to rise when you serve up these blue cheesy potatoes.

6   *large baking potatoes, scrubbed and dried*
3   *tablespoons butter*
½   *cup sour cream*
¼   *cup crumbled blue cheese*
     *Salt and pepper to taste*
4   *scallions, finely minced*
     *Paprika*

**1**   Bake potatoes in preheated 425-degree oven for 45 to 60 minutes, until soft.

**2**   Cut a slice off the top of each potato. Scoop out insides into a bowl, being careful not to break the shells. Place shells on baking pan; set aside.

**3**   Add butter to the scooped potatoes; mash together well. Beat in sour cream.

**4**   Press blue cheese through a strainer into the potato mixture. Beat well. Add salt and pepper.

**5**   Fill gun with potato mixture. Fit with decorator tip.

**6**   Using gun at high speed, pipe potatoes into the reserved shells, filling each half full. Sprinkle with scallions; cover with balance of potatoes. Sprinkle tops lightly with paprika.

**7**   Return to preheated 425-degree oven and bake for about 15 minutes, until lightly browned and hot.

6 servings.

## Duchesse Potato Rings

6   *medium potatoes, peeled and quartered*
2   *whole eggs*
2   *egg yolks*
3   *tablespoons butter*
1   *teaspoon salt*
⅛   *teaspoon white pepper*
⅛   *teaspoon nutmeg*
     *Paprika*

**1**   Cook potatoes in boiling salted water to cover until soft but still firm.

**2**   Drain potatoes well; put them through a food mill or potato ricer. Beat with a wooden spoon until smooth.

**3**   Lightly beat together eggs and egg yolks; combine with mashed potatoes. Add butter, salt, pepper and nutmeg; whip until fluffy.

**4**   Fill gun with potato mixture. Fit with decorator tip.

**5**   Using gun at high speed, pipe mixture into 3-inch rings on a greased baking sheet. (Make 2 rings per serving.) Sprinkle lightly with paprika.

**6**   Bake in preheated 450-degree oven for 10 to 15 minutes, until browned and hot.

6 to 8 servings.

# Stuffed Cauliflower

This modest vegetable loses its inhibitions and blossoms into a sophisticated showpiece.

*1  large cauliflower*

*½  recipe for Pâte à Choux (see page 57)*

*1  tablespoon caraway seeds*

*2  tablespoons grated Parmesan cheese*

*1  teaspoon salt*

*3  tablespoons melted butter*

*¼  cup packaged bread crumbs*

**1**   Trim cauliflower by removing outer leaves and part of core. Cut off any blemishes.

**2**   Place in covered saucepan; boil in salted water to cover for 15 minutes. Drain in colander.

**3**   Carefully remove enough of the center flowerets to fill 1 cup, leaving a hollow, sturdy shell. Mash flowerets with a fork; set aside. Place shell in well greased casserole.

**4**   Prepare Pâte à Choux as directed, through step 2.

**5**   Add mashed cauliflower, caraway seeds, 1 tablespoon Parmesan and salt to Pâte à Choux; mix well.

**6**   Fill gun with mixture. Fit with decorator tip.

**7**   Using gun at high speed, pipe mixture into cauliflower shell, making swirls at the top.

**8**   Drizzle butter over the stuffed shell; sprinkle with a mixture of bread crumbs and remaining Parmesan.

**9**   Bake in preheated 375-degree oven for 50 to 55 minutes.

6 servings.

# Desserts

# Desserts

" 'Tis the Dessert that graces all the Feast, For an ill end disparages all the rest." If you read restaurant menus from bottom to top, you're in good company. A lot of people consider dessert the most important part of the meal (and the meal merely the straightest line to dessert). When they're your guests, why not indulge them?

Cream puffs, éclairs, parfaits, cream pies, cakes — they're fun to make with the foodgun, and they look and taste superb. Try embellishing your creations with whipped cream rosettes or stars; pipe out luscious meringue peaks; create beautiful trims and borders. With a little practice, you can become an expert in the art of cake decorating.

Preparing Ahead: Most of the desserts here will taste just fine if they're prepared a day or two in advance and stored in the refrigerator.

You can freeze the following: cakes, whipped cream, fillings and toppings that do not contain gelatin, and unfilled pie shells and pastry horns.

Don't freeze: meringues, filled pies, fruits, or foods containing gelatin.

## Cheddar Flowers on Fruit

Flowers that are literally good enough to eat.

4  cups fresh fruit, cut up
5  ounces sharp Cheddar cheese
      (crock type)

**1**   Place fruit in a glass bowl or low casserole. Refrigerate.

**2**   Let cheese sit out of refrigerator for ½ hour.

**3**   Fill gun with cheese. Fit with flower or star disc.

**4**   Using gun at high speed, press flowers onto waxed paper-lined baking pan. Follow directions for making pressed cookies (see page 9).

**5**   Refrigerate Cheddar flowers until firm. Remove from waxed paper and distribute over top of fruit.

Makes 12 Cheddar flowers.

## Brandy Snaps

¼  cup light corn syrup
¼  cup molasses
½  cup butter
 1  cup all-purpose flour
⅔  cup granulated sugar
 1  teaspoon ground ginger
 2  teaspoons brandy
 1  teaspoon grated lemon rind
1½  cups heavy cream
¼  cup confectioners' sugar, sifted

**1**   Heat syrup and molasses to boiling. Remove from heat; add butter and stir.

**2**   Sift together flour, sugar and ginger. Add gradually to molasses mixture, while stirring. Add brandy and lemon rind. Mix well.

**3**   Drop by teaspoonsful three inches apart on greased cookie sheets.

**4**   Bake for 14 to 15 minutes in preheated 300-degree oven.

**5**   Remove from oven. Quickly loosen one cookie at a time and roll over ¾-inch diameter wooden dowel (or handle of a wooden spoon). Form flutes or cylinders. (If cookies harden before shaping, reheat in oven for 1 or 2 minutes to soften.) Gently remove from dowel and cool on wire rack.

**6**   Whip heavy cream with confectioners' sugar until stiff.

**7**   Fill gun with whipped cream. Fit with decorator tip.

**8**   Using gun at low speed, pipe cream into both ends of each cookie.

Makes about 2 dozen brandy snaps.

# Cream Horns

One of the lightest of pastries is this flaky, butter-rich product. It also can be used to make patty shells and is hard to tell apart from professional puff pastry.

   3  *cups all-purpose flour*
   2  *cups butter (cut into large pieces), softened*
   1  *cup sour cream*
5½ *-inch cream horn tubes*
   1  *egg, beaten*
       *Granulated sugar*
   2  *cups heavy cream*
   6  *tablespoons confectioners' sugar, sifted*
   2  *teaspoons vanilla extract*

**1**   Place flour in a large bowl. Add butter. Using fingers or pastry blender, blend until mixture resembles coarse corn meal. Stir in sour cream; blend thoroughly.

**2**   Shape into rectangle. Cut into 4 equal pieces. Completely cover each piece with plastic wrap and refrigerate for 3 to 4 hours.

**3**   On a floured surface, roll pastry until it is ⅛-inch thick. Cut into strips 30 inches long and ¾-inch wide.

**4**   Beginning at the narrowest end of a cream horn tube, wind a strip of dough around it, making sure that the pastry edges slightly overlap each other. Repeat with each tube.

**5**   Brush top and sides (not bottom) of pastry horns with egg. Sprinkle brushed parts with granulated sugar.

**6**   Place on ungreased baking pan 1 inch apart. Bake in preheated 400-degree oven for about 20 minutes until golden brown. Remove tubes from pastry immediately; place pastry horns on wire rack to cool.

**7**   Whip heavy cream with confectioners' sugar and vanilla until stiff.

**8**   Fill gun with cream. Fit with decorator tip.

**9**   Using gun at high speed, pipe cream into cooled pastry horns. Refrigerate.

Makes about 1½ dozen cream horns.

*Shown right, Gazpacho Mold (p. 73), Baked Zucchini Boats (p. 91), Coquilles Saint-Jacques (p. 79).*

*Blue Cheese Potatoes (p. 93).*

# Cream Puffs

1 cup water
½ cup butter
¼ teaspoon salt
1 cup sifted all-purpose flour
4 large eggs
Pastry Cream or Crème Saint-Honoré
(recipes appear on next page)

**1** Place water, butter and salt in a saucepan and bring to a boil. Turn off heat; stir in flour all at once. Beat well until mixture forms a mass and leaves sides of pan.

**2** Cool for 1 minute. Add eggs one at a time, beating well after each addition. Mixture should be smooth and glossy.

**3** Fill gun with mixture. Fit with decorator tip.

**4** Using gun at low speed, pipe 1½-inch mounds of dough onto greased baking sheet 2 inches apart.

**5** Bake for 15 minutes in preheated 450-degree oven. Reduce heat to 350 degrees and continue baking for another 30 minutes until shells are nicely browned and sides are dry and rigid. Make a slit in the side of each puff with a small sharp knife. Remove from pan and cool on wire rack.

**6** Cut a cap off each puff. Fill shells with Pastry Cream or Crème Saint-Honoré. Replace caps.

Makes 12 to 15 medium large cream puffs.

------

**Eclairs:** Pipe 3-inch lengths of dough onto greased baking sheet. Fill baked shells with whipped cream, Pastry Cream or Crème Saint-Honoré. Makes 12 to 15 éclairs.

## Making Cream Puff Swans

**1** Prepare cream puff dough as directed above through step 2. Refrigerate for at least 2 hours.

**2** To make swans' necks: Butter a baking sheet. Using your index finger, draw outlines in the butter for 10 question-marks, each 3 inches long. Space them 1 inch apart.

**3** Fill gun with dough. Fit with decorator tip.

**4** Use gun at low speed. By pressing trigger gently and immediately releasing, make dough flow slowly out of foodgun, following the outlines on the baking sheet.

**5** Bake in preheated 450-degree oven for 12 minutes. Remove from pan; cool on wire rack.

**6** To make swans' bodies: Pipe balance of dough into ten 1½-inch mounds 2 inches apart on greased baking pans. Bake as for medium large cream puffs (see step 5 in preceding recipe).

**7** When puffs are cool, cut a cap off each. Reserve caps. Pipe whipped cream into the bottom shells, mounding high. Insert a question-mark neck into the cream at the edge of each shell.

**8** To make swans' wings: Cut a reserved cap in half; place both halves on top of whipped cream, on each side of the swan's neck, leaving a small space between the wings. Repeat with each swan. Sprinkle swans with confectioners' sugar.

## Pastry Cream
(crème pâtisserie)

    5 large egg yolks
    ¾ cup granulated sugar
    ⅔ cup all-purpose flour
    2 cups milk
    1 tablespoon butter
1½ tablespoons vanilla extract

**1**  In a heavy saucepan, combine egg yolks and sugar; beat just until well blended. Beat in flour.

**2**  Slowly pour milk into egg mixture, stirring constantly. Cook over medium low heat, stirring constantly, until mixture boils. Reduce heat to low; cook, stirring, for 2 more minutes.

**3**  Remove pan from heat; stir in butter. Add vanilla and beat well. Cool and refrigerate.

Makes about 2½ cups.

———

*Variations:* Pastry cream may be flavored as desired. Eliminate vanilla when making variations. *Chocolate Cream*—Add 2 ounces melted semi-sweet chocolate and 1 tablespoon orange-flavored liqueur. *Coffee Cream*—Add 1½ teaspoons instant coffee and 1 tablespoon coffee-flavored liqueur.

———

*Note:* Egg whites may be saved for meringues or Crème Saint-Honoré. Store whites in freezer.

## Crème Saint-Honoré

8 large egg whites
3 tablespoons granulated sugar
  Pastry Cream (see recipe this page)

**1**  Beat egg whites until they form soft peaks. Gradually beat in sugar; continue beating until stiff and glossy.

**2**  Fold egg white mixture into *hot* Pastry Cream. Cool and refrigerate.

Makes about 8 cups.

———

*Note:* Egg yolks may be saved to make egg custard. Refrigerate unbroken yolks in jar with water to cover.

# Gâteau Saint-Honoré

½ recipe for Short Pastry
 (see page 118)

 Pâte à Choux (see recipe, page 57)

 Caramel (recipe appears on next page)

 Crème Saint-Honoré (see recipe,
 page 102)

½ cup heavy cream

1½ tablespoons confectioners' sugar

 Red and green glacéed cherries

**1** Prepare Short Pastry as directed. Roll dough into an 8-inch disc slightly thicker than ⅛ inch. Place on a lightly greased baking sheet. Using an 8-inch round baking pan as a guide, trim the disc. Prick dough with a fork at ½-inch intervals.

**2** Bake in preheated 400-degree oven for 15 to 20 minutes, until lightly browned. Cool on wire rack.

**3** Prepare Pâte à Choux as directed through step 2.

**4** Fill gun with Pâte à Choux. Fit with decorator tip.

**5** Using gun at low speed, pipe dough into 12 walnut-size mounds 2 inches apart on a lightly greased baking sheet. Reserve remaining dough. Bake puffs in a preheated 450-degree oven for 15 minutes. Reduce heat to 350 degrees and continue baking for another 10 minutes. Make a slit in the side of each puff with a small sharp knife so steam can escape. Remove from pan; cool on wire rack.

**6** Butter a baking sheet and trace an 8-inch circle in the butter, using a round baking pan as a guide. Pipe remaining Pâte à Choux onto the traced circle with the foodgun, forming a ring. Bake in preheated 450-degree oven for 15 minutes. Reduce heat to 350 degrees; continue baking for another 30 minutes until browned. Make several slits in side with small sharp knife. Remove from pan; cool on wire rack.

**7** Prepare caramel as directed. (Caramel hardens quickly, so be prepared to work fast when it is ready.) Place pastry disc on a serving plate; drizzle a ring of caramel around the edge of the pastry; place Pâte à Choux ring firmly on top.

**8** Tilt caramel pan and dip tops and bottoms of puffs in the caramel. Place puffs firmly on top of Pâte à Choux ring, spacing evenly. Reserve one puff.

**9** Prepare Crème Saint-Honoré as directed, using 5 egg whites instead of the usual 8. Fill gun with the cream. Fit with filler tip.

**10** Using gun at low speed, press tip into each puff and fill with cream.

**11** Spoon remaining Crème Saint-Honoré into center of the Pâte à Choux ring, smoothing gently. Place reserved puff in the middle.

**12** Whip heavy cream with sugar until stiff.

**13** Fill gun with whipped cream. Fit with decorator tip.

**14** Use gun at low speed. Decorate as desired. (Refer to cover photo.) Place alternating red and green glacéed cherries around inside edge of the Gâteau.

8 to 10 servings.

## Caramel

1 cup granulated sugar
¼ cup cold water
⅛ teaspoon cream of tartar

Place ingredients in saucepan. Cook over medium high heat, washing down any sugar sticking to sides of pan with a brush dipped in cold water, until mixture is a light caramel color. Remove from heat.

## Mont Blanc aux Marrons

A magic mountain . . . buttery chestnut purée, sparkled with cognac, under whirl upon whirl of whipped cream.

1 cup butter, softened
15-ounce can sweetened chestnut purée
2 tablespoons cognac
1½ cups heavy cream
3 tablespoons confectioners' sugar, sifted
1½ teaspoons vanilla extract

**1** Cream butter. Add chestnut purée and cognac; blend thoroughly. Cover and refrigerate for 3 hours.

**2** Fill gun with purée. Fit with filler tip.

**3** Use gun at high speed. Pipe out mixture, letting it fall at random into greased 8-inch ring mold, forming a nest-like effect.

**4** Immediately turn out on a serving plate and refrigerate.

**5** Whip heavy cream with confectioners' sugar and vanilla until stiff.

**6** Fill center of chestnut nest with a mountain of whipped cream.

10 small servings (it's very rich).

# Chocolate Roll
## aux Marrons

A superb chestnut filling. Lovely to behold, even better to eat. And easy to prepare.

6 *ounces semi-sweet chocolate squares*

3 *tablespoons strong coffee*

6 *large eggs, separated*

¾ *cup granulated sugar*

1 *teaspoon vanilla extract*

2 *cups heavy cream*

¼ *cup confectioners' sugar, sifted*

2 *teaspoons rum*

10-ounce *jar marron pieces (chestnuts) in syrup*

*Additional confectioners' sugar*

**1**   Melt chocolate with coffee over hot water. Cool slightly.

**2**   With mixer on medium to high speed, beat egg yolks until light and lemon colored. Gradually beat in sugar; continue beating until so thick that ribbon forms on surface when mixture falls from beater. (This may take about 10 minutes.)

**3**   Add melted chocolate to egg yolk mixture; stir thoroughly. Mix in vanilla.

**4**   Beat egg whites until stiff. Fold into chocolate mixture.

**5**   Grease a 10 x 15-inch jelly roll pan. Line with waxed paper; grease the paper. Pour batter into pan and spread gently with rubber spatula.

**6**   Bake in preheated 350-degree oven for 15 minutes. Cool on wire rack for about 20 minutes.

**7**   Whip heavy cream with confectioners' sugar and rum until very stiff. Reserve 1 cup of whipped cream for decorating.

**8**   Drain marrons; break them into small pieces, reserving 3 or 4 choice large marrons.

**9**   Add small marron pieces to whipped cream; mix gently. Spread over cake.

**10**   Starting from short side, roll cake by lifting away waxed paper underneath it to start cake rolling forward. Roll quickly and gently onto serving platter. (This cake tends to crack a little as it rolls.)

**11**   Fill gun with reserved cup of whipped cream. Fit with decorator tip.

**12**   Using gun at low speed, decorate top of cake with rosettes. Place reserved marrons on rosettes. Sift confectioners' sugar over entire cake.

10 servings.

# Viennese Apricot
# Rice Ring

A dessert that combines old-fashioned wholesomeness with sophistication.

   2   envelopes unflavored gelatin
   1   cup cold water
1½   cups long grain rice
   5   cups milk
   ½   cup granulated sugar
   2   teaspoons vanilla extract
2½   cups heavy cream
   ¾   cup apricot preserves
30-ounce can apricot halves, drained
        Apricot Sauce (recipe follows)
1½   tablespoons confectioners' sugar,
        sifted

**1**   Sprinkle gelatin over cold water to soften. Set aside.

**2**   Cook rice and milk over boiling water for 15 minutes. Stir in sugar; continue cooking for another hour over simmering water, stirring occasionally, until rice is tender and most of the milk has been absorbed.

**3**   Remove rice from heat. Stir in gelatin and vanilla; mix thoroughly. Set mixture over a bowl of ice water to cool. Stir occasionally to prevent it from setting.

**4**   Whip 2 cups of the heavy cream until stiff. Fold into cooled rice mixture.

**5**   Pour half the rice mixture into a 2½-quart ring mold; cover with apricot preserves. Do not let preserves touch sides of pan. Fill with balance of rice mixture. Refrigerate for 5 to 6 hours.

**6**   Dip mold quickly into warm water; unmold onto serving platter with a lip.

**7**   Fill center of mold with drained apricots, reserving 6 to 8 halves for garnish.

**8**   Spoon cold Apricot Sauce into bottom of platter but not over rice ring. Also spoon some sauce over apricots in center of mold. Put leftover sauce in serving bowl and set aside. Arrange reserved apricots around top of rice ring, rounded side up.

**9**   Whip remaining heavy cream with confectioners' sugar until stiff.

**10**   Fill gun with whipped cream. Fit with decorator tip.

**11**   Using gun at low speed, pipe rosettes on top of each apricot. Serve with reserved Apricot Sauce.

12 to 14 servings.

## Apricot Sauce

   2   12-ounce jars apricot preserves
   ¾   cup canned apricot nectar
   3   tablespoons brandy

In a saucepan, heat preserves over low heat until soft enough to stir. Add nectar and brandy; stir well. Remove from heat. Refrigerate until ready to serve.

# Surprise
# de Boule Etoilée

A star-studded scene-stealer. A blissful blending of cream . . . each mouthful a sweet surprise. And the best surprise— it's easy to make.

16  *double lady fingers*

 4  *tablespoons cooking sherry*

½  *cup butter, softened*

 1  *cup plus 3 tablespoons confectioners' sugar, sifted*

 2  *large eggs, separated*

½  *cup chopped toasted almonds*

 1  *cup macaroon crumbs*

 2  *cups heavy cream*

**1**   Line a 1½-quart bowl that is 3½ inches deep with aluminum foil, fitting it to the shape of the bowl and folding it over the outer edge.

**2**   Split the lady fingers and line bottom and sides of bowl with them. Fill in all spaces, cutting lady fingers to fit if necessary. Reserve remaining lady fingers. Brush lady fingers in bowl with 2 tablespoons sherry. Cover bowl; set aside.

**3**   With mixer at medium to high speed, cream butter with 1 cup sugar until light and fluffy. Add egg yolks one at a time, beating well after each addition. Add almonds, macaroon crumbs and remaining sherry; mix thoroughly.

**4**   Beat egg whites until stiff. Beat 1 cup heavy cream until stiff.

**5**   Fold egg whites and whipped cream into mixture.

**6**   Fill bowl containing lady fingers with almond cream mixture; cover with layer of remaining lady fingers, completely encasing cream. Cover and refrigerate for several hours.

**7**   Unmold onto serving platter; remove aluminum foil.

**8**   Whip remaining cup of heavy cream with 3 tablespoons confectioners' sugar until stiff.

**9**   Fill gun with whipped cream. Fit with decorator tip.

**10**   Using gun at low speed, pipe small whipped cream stars over entire surface of lady finger ball. Refrigerate until ready to serve.

10 servings.

## Company
## Berry Baskets

These versatile baskets may be frozen, defrosted and crisped in the oven for 5 minutes before filling. They can be filled with fruits, vegetables, fish or meats.

 2  cups all-purpose flour, sifted
 ¾  teaspoon salt
 1  cup butter, softened
 3  tablespoons ice water
 1  cup water
 1  teaspoon almond extract
 4  large eggs
1½  cups heavy cream
 ½  cup plus 3 tablespoons confectioners' sugar, sifted
 1  teaspoon vanilla extract
 2  pints fresh strawberries, raspberries or blueberries

**1**  Sift 1 cup flour with ¼ teaspoon salt into bowl; add ½ cup butter. Blend together using fingers or pastry blender until mixture resembles coarse corn meal. Add ice water. Gather dough together into a ball; divide into 8 equal pieces.

**2**  Cut out a 3-inch circle of waxed paper. Using it as a guide, pat each piece of dough into a 3-inch round on an ungreased cookie sheet. Prick each round in several places with a fork.

**3**  Place 1 cup of water, the remaining ½ cup butter and ½ teaspoon salt into saucepan; bring to a boil. Turn off heat. Stir in almond extract and remaining cup flour all at once. Beat well until mixture forms a mass and leaves sides of pan.

**4**  Cool for 1 minute. Add eggs, one at a time, beating well after each addition until smooth and glossy.

**5**  Fill gun with dough. Fit with decorator tip.

**6**  Using gun at low speed, pipe 8 or 9 star mounds around the edge of each pastry circle, forming a basket with a 1-inch high rim.

**7**  Bake in preheated 400-degree oven for 30 to 35 minutes, until puffed rim is firm and nicely browned.

**8**  Remove from cookie sheet and cool on wire rack.

**9**  Whip heavy cream with 3 tablespoons of the confectioners' sugar and vanilla until stiff.

**10**  Wash and hull berries. In blender, whirl ½ pint of the berries with remaining ½ cup confectioners' sugar.

**11**  Fill pastry baskets with whipped cream; top with remaining 1½ pints of berries; drizzle with sugar berry mixture.

Makes 8 dessert baskets.

---

*Variation:* Pastry baskets may be filled with chicken, ham, mushrooms, etc., and served for lunch or as an appetizer.

# Pistachio Cream
# Meringue

This is a true Bavarian cream with a lovely, velvety texture. By itself it makes a luscious dessert. Coupled with the meringue shell, it is fit for royalty.

Large Meringue Shell (recipe follows)
1   envelope unflavored gelatin
¼   cup cold water
6   large egg yolks (reserve whites for
        Meringue Shell)
¾   cup granulated sugar
2   cups milk
1   teaspoon vanilla extract
½   cup finely chopped unsalted pistachio
        nuts
2   tablespoons Kirsch
6   drops green food coloring
1   cup heavy cream
    Additional chopped pistachio nuts

**1**   Prepare Meringue Shell as directed.

**2**   Sprinkle gelatin over cold water to soften. Set aside.

**3**   In heavy saucepan, combine egg yolks with sugar; mix thoroughly with wire whisk. Stir in milk. Cook over medium low heat, stirring constantly with a wooden spoon until mixture thinly coats the spoon. (Don't let it simmer or boil.)

**4**   Remove from heat; stir for another minute. Add vanilla and mix. Add gelatin, stirring well. Add pistachio nuts, Kirsch and green coloring; mix well. Cool at room temperature for about 20 minutes. Refrigerate until thick and just about to set.

**5**   Whip heavy cream until stiff; fold into chilled pistachio cream mixture.

**6**   Place baked Meringue Shell on serving platter. Fill with cream. Sprinkle with additional nuts.

**7**   Spoon any extra pistachio cream into individual serving dishes.

8 to 10 servings.


**Large Meringue Shell**

6   large egg whites
        (reserve yolks for Pistachio Cream)
1   cup granulated sugar

**1**   Trace 8-inch circle in center of a lightly greased baking sheet.

**2**   With mixer at medium to high speed, beat egg whites until foamy or until soft peaks begin to form. Very gradually add sugar, beating constantly until stiff and glossy.

**3**   Spread a ¼-inch layer of meringue inside the traced circle, forming the bottom of the meringue shell.

**4**   Fill gun with the remaining meringue. Fit gun with decorator tip.

**5**   Using gun at low speed, form sides of shell by piping out attached high mounds of meringue around the edge of the circle.

**6**   Bake in preheated 250-degree oven for 1½ hours. Turn off heat and leave meringue shell in oven for another hour. Remove to wire rack.

## Orange Ambrosia Meringue

Juicy orange slices, laced with liqueur, crunched with coconut and frothed with meringue. And low in calories!

    8  eating oranges
  1/3  cup orange liqueur (Triple Sec or
         Cointreau)
  1/2  cup orange juice
  3/4  cup flaked coconut
       Meringue Topping (see recipe,
         page 127)

**1**  Peel oranges with knife, removing white membrane. Slice in rounds.

**2**  Mix orange liqueur with orange juice.

**3**  In a 1 1/2 -quart soufflé dish, place alternate layers of orange slices and coconut, beginning and ending with oranges. Pour some of the liqueur mixture over each layer of orange slices.

**4**  Fill gun with Meringue Topping. Fit with decorator tip.

**5**  With gun at low speed, pipe 2-inch high peaks on top of oranges, starting from the edges of the dish and working towards center. (This prevents meringue from shrinking.)

**6**  Bake in preheated 425-degree oven for 4 to 6 minutes. Cool on rack for 1 hour at room temperature.

**7**  Refrigerate until ready to serve.

8 servings.

## Frozen Rum Raisin Parfaits

Perfectly delectable, and perfectly easy to make. Keep them handy in your freezer for unexpected guests.

  1/2  cup finely chopped raisins
  1/2  cup dark rum
    2  cups heavy cream
  1/2  cup chopped almonds
  1/2  cup soft macaroon crumbs
1 1/2  pints vanilla ice cream, softened
    3  tablespoons confectioners' sugar,
         sifted
       Additional chopped almonds

**1**  Soak chopped raisins in rum for 1 hour.

**2**  Whip 1 cup of the heavy cream until stiff.

**3**  Fold rum raisin mixture, almonds and macaroon crumbs into whipped cream.

**4**  Stir mixture into softened ice cream; mix thoroughly.

**5**  Spoon into 8 parfait glasses until each is 2/3 full. Freeze.

**6**  Whip remaining cup of heavy cream with 3 tablespoons sugar until stiff.

**7**  Fill gun with whipped cream. Fit with decorator tip.

**8**  Using gun at low speed, pipe cream into top third of parfait glasses, swirling and mounding high. Sprinkle with chopped almonds and freeze. Serve as a frozen dessert.

8 servings.

# Cold Lime Soufflé

A lime lover's lure.

> 5 large eggs, separated
> 1 cup granulated sugar
> 2 tablespoons grated lime rind
> ½ cup lime juice
> ⅛ teaspoon salt
> 1 envelope unflavored gelatin
> ¼ cup rum
> 5 or 6 drops green food coloring
> 1½ cups heavy cream
> ¼ cup toasted coconut (optional)
> 1 tablespoon confectioners' sugar, sifted

**1** Prepare a 1-quart soufflé dish with a paper collar. (See directions this page.)

**2** With mixer at medium to high speed, beat egg yolks until light and fluffy. Add ½ cup sugar; beat until thick enough for ribbon to form on surface when mixture falls from beater. (This may take about 10 minutes.) Add grated lime rind, lime juice and salt; stir.

**3** Place mixture in heavy saucepan; stir constantly over low heat until thick enough to coat a wooden spoon. Do not boil. Remove from heat.

**4** Sprinkle gelatin over rum to soften; add to egg yolk mixture, stirring until gelatin is dissolved. Add food coloring and stir well. Transfer mixture to a large bowl and cool, stirring occasionally.

**5** Beat egg whites until foamy. Gradually add remaining ½ cup sugar, beating until stiff and glossy. Fold into yolk mixture.

**6** Beat 1 cup of the heavy cream until soft peaks form. Fold into egg mixture. Pour into prepared soufflé dish and refrigerate for 4 to 5 hours. (It's best when soufflé is very cold.)

**7** Remove from refrigerator. Sprinkle top of soufflé with toasted coconut (optional).

**8** Carefully remove paper collar.

**9** Whip remaining ½ cup heavy cream with confectioners' sugar until stiff.

**10** Fill gun with whipped cream. Fit with decorator tip.

**11** Using gun at low speed, pipe rosettes around top edge of soufflé. Place 1 rosette in center.

8 servings.

### Making a Collar for a Soufflé Dish

Tear off a long piece of waxed paper, fold it in half lengthwise, and wrap it around the outside of the soufflé dish. (Secure it by tying a string around it.) The paper should extend 4 to 5 inches above the top of the dish, like a stand-up collar. Brush the exposed inside edge of the paper with vegetable oil.

## Coconut Orange Glace

An extremely simple dessert to make, and worthy of very special company.

- *1 large egg white*
- *½ cup granulated sugar*
- *1 cup heavy cream*
- *2 teaspoons grated orange rind*
- *¼ cup flaked coconut, toasted*
  *Additional flaked coconut, toasted*

**1** Beat egg white until soft peaks form. Gradually add ¼ cup sugar, beating until stiff and glossy.

**2** Whip heavy cream with remaining ¼ cup sugar until stiff. Fold into egg white. Then fold in orange rind and coconut.

**3** Fill gun with mixture. Fit with decorator tip.

**4** With gun at high speed, pipe mixture into serving cups (½ -cup capacity), forming decorative mounds. Garnish with additional coconut.

**5** Freeze. Serve as a frozen dessert.

6 to 8 servings.

## Frozen Ricotta and Nesselrode

Ricotta and Nesselrode mix and merge in minutes to make a fanciful freeze-for-later splurge.

- *2 15-ounce containers whole milk ricotta cheese*
- *10-ounce jar Nesselrode*
- *2 tablespoons confectioners' sugar, sifted*
- *1 tablespoon grated semi-sweet chocolate squares*

**1** Set aside 1 cup of ricotta. Place remaining cheese in bowl. Add Nesselrode, reserving 6 pieces for garnishing. Mix together thoroughly.

**2** Fill 6 dessert dishes or parfait glasses with mixture.

**3** To make topping, place reserved cup of ricotta in a bowl. Add sugar and chocolate; mix thoroughly.

**4** Fill gun with topping. Fit with decorator tip.

**5** Using gun at high speed, pipe swirls of topping on each serving. Place a reserved piece of Nesselrode in center of each swirl. Freeze.

**6** Remove from freezer ½ hour before serving.

6 servings.

# Ice Cream Cake

Start with two kinds of ice cream, add all kinds of other goodies like almonds and macaroons . . . end up with a delightful confection that will bring down the house.

   1   quart pistachio ice cream, slightly softened

 24   macaroons, crumbled

   1   cup chopped almonds

   2   ounces semi-sweet chocolate squares, chopped

   1   quart chocolate ice cream, slightly softened

   1   cup heavy cream

   2   tablespoons confectioners' sugar, sifted

1½   teaspoons unsweetened cocoa, sifted

**1**   Line bottom of an 8-inch spring form pan with waxed paper. Spread pistachio ice cream across the bottom.

**2**   Mix macaroons, almonds and chocolate together. Spread half this mixture over the pistachio ice cream.

**3**   Spread chocolate ice cream over macaroon layer. Spread remaining macaroon mixture on top, pressing it into the ice cream so there are no loose crumbs, nuts or chocolate.

**4**   Freeze for at least 4 hours, or until hard.

**5**   Whip heavy cream with sugar and cocoa until very stiff.

**6**   Invert ice cream cake onto serving platter. Remove sides of pan; lift off bottom of pan and waxed paper.

**7**   Fill gun with whipped cream. Fit with decorator tip.

**8**   Using gun at high speed, pipe design over top of cake. Refreeze until 15 minutes before serving.

8 to 10 servings.

------

*Variation:* Any combination of ice cream flavors may be substituted, such as coffee and vanilla fudge, or peach and chocolate chip mint.

# Mint Chip
# Mousse

Its cool, refreshing beauty will earn you a mint of compliments.

   *7-ounce box mint patties*
   *1  envelope unflavored gelatin*
*¼  cup cold water*
   *3  large eggs*
*¾  cup granulated sugar*
   *2  teaspoons mint extract*
   *1  tablespoon crème de menthe*
   *4  to 6 drops green food coloring*
*1¼  cups heavy cream*

**1**   Reserve 6 mint patties. Cut balance of patties into ¼-inch pieces.

**2**   Sprinkle gelatin over cold water to soften. Stir over hot water until dissolved. Set aside.

**3**   With mixer at medium to high speed, beat eggs until foamy. Add sugar; beat for about 10 minutes until very thick. Add mint extract and crème de menthe; beat well. Add food coloring and stir to distribute evenly.

**4**   Add cooled but unset gelatin to egg mixture. Stir well.

**5**   Whip heavy cream until stiff. Reserve about ½ cup of whipped cream for garnish. Fold the rest into egg mixture when it is about to set.

**6**   Fold mint patty pieces gently into mixture.

**7**   Spoon into 5- to 6-cup serving dish. Refrigerate.

**8**   Arrange reserved whole patties on top of mousse.

**9**   Fill gun with reserved whipped cream. Fit with decorator tip.

**10**   Using gun at low speed, pipe 6 rosettes of cream on top of each patty.

6 to 8 servings.

# Chocolate
# Moussed Pears

Pair two pear halves with chocolate mousse . . . the result is sheer perfection.

2  29-ounce cans of pear halves

2  cups heavy cream

¼  cup confectioners' sugar, sifted

2  teaspoons vanilla extract

   Chocolate Mousse (recipe follows)

**1**  Drain pears and pat dry.

**2**  Whip heavy cream with sugar and vanilla until stiff. Transfer to a large glass serving dish with a lip, or divide mixture and place in 2 stemmed cake stands with lips.

**3**  Arrange ½ of the pear halves on waxed paper, rounded side down. Spoon a generous amount of the firm Chocolate Mousse into each pear half. Top with an additional pear half.

**4**  Fill gun with balance of mousse. Fit with decorator tip.

**5**  Take one filled pear at a time and place it stem end up on the waxed paper. Using gun at high speed, pipe chocolate mousse all along the exposed seams of the pear. Place each pear in whipped cream, stem end up. Refrigerate until ready to serve.

7 to 10 servings.

## Chocolate Mousse

4 ounces unsweetened chocolate squares, melted

½  cup butter, softened

1½  cups confectioners' sugar, sifted

2  large eggs, separated

1  tablespoon rum

1  cup heavy cream

**1**  Melt chocolate over hot water. Set aside to cool.

**2**  With mixer at medium to high speed, cream butter with 1 cup of sugar. Add egg yolks one at a time, beating well after each addition. Add rum and mix. Add cooled chocolate; beat well.

**3**  Beat egg whites until stiff.

**4**  Beat 1 cup of heavy cream with remaining ½ cup sugar until stiff.

**5**  Fold egg whites and whipped cream into chocolate mixture. Refrigerate to firm. (Mousse is ready to use when it's firm but not hard.)

# French Crullers

Golden doughnuts . . . with a French twist.

   3 tablespoons butter, softened
 ½ cup granulated sugar
   2 large eggs
1¾ cups all-purpose flour
   2 teaspoons baking powder
 ½ teaspoon salt
 ¼ teaspoon nutmeg
 ¼ cup light cream or half and half
   1 teaspoon vanilla extract
     Vegetable oil for frying
     Confectioners' sugar

**1** With beater on medium to high speed, cream butter and sugar until light and fluffy. Add eggs one at a time; beat after each addition.

**2** Sift together flour, baking powder, salt and nutmeg. Add flour mixture alternately with cream and vanilla to egg sugar mixture. Stir well.

**3** Cover dough; refrigerate for 3 hours.

**4** Fill a deep fryer or 3-quart saucepan ⅔ full of vegetable oil.

**5** Cut out rounds of brown paper (from grocery bags, etc.) slightly smaller than the circumference of the fryer.

**6** Grease each round of paper on one side with solid shortening.

**7** Heat oil to 375 degrees on deep-fat thermometer.

**8** Fill gun with dough. Fit with decorator tip.

**9** Using gun at high speed, pipe S-shaped squiggles or rings 2 inches in diameter onto greased sides of paper.

**10** Invert paper rounds into the fryer. The doughnuts should release themselves from the paper. Remove paper with tongs and discard. Each paper round should be used only once.

**11** Fry doughnuts until golden brown on first side; turn over. When browned on both sides, remove with slotted spoon or tongs. Place on paper towels or brown paper to drain.

**12** Roll in confectioners' sugar.

Makes 2 dozen doughnuts.

# Decorated Cup Cakes

Fine-textured "cakelettes" . . . individually decorated.

½ cup butter, softened

1 cup granulated sugar

1 teaspoon vanilla extract

2 large eggs

¼ teaspoon salt

1 teaspoon baking powder

1 teaspoon baking soda

2 cups all-purpose flour

1 cup sour cream

Icing Cream Decorations (recipe and instructions follow)

**1** With beater at medium to high speed, cream butter with sugar until light and fluffy. Add vanilla and eggs; beat well.

**2** Sift together dry ingredients. Add alternately with sour cream to egg butter mixture. Beat well after each addition.

**3** Grease cup cake pans; fill each cup ⅔ full. Bake in preheated 350-degree oven for 20 to 25 minutes, until cake tester comes out clean. Remove from pans and cool on wire rack.

**4** Arrange Icing Cream Decorations on cup cakes.

Makes about 2 dozen regular or 4 dozen miniature cup cakes.

## Icing Cream

With this basic recipe, you can master the art of cake decorating.

¾ cup butter (not too yellow in color), softened

¼ cup white shortening

1 teaspoon vanilla extract

1 pound confectioners' sugar, sifted

Assorted food colors

**1** With mixer at medium to high speed, cream butter, shortening and vanilla with sugar. Beat just enough to mix thoroughly. Mixture should not become greasy.

**2** If you want icing creams of different colors, divide mixture. Add a few drops of desired color to each batch, stirring well so color is evenly distributed.

**3** Refrigerate for 2 hours.

### Making Decorations With Icing Cream

**1** Remove cream from refrigerator ½ hour before using.

**2** Fill gun with cream. Fit with desired disc.

**3** Using gun at high speed, press decorations onto waxed paper. Store in freezer.

**4** When decorations are needed, remove them from waxed paper and arrange on cakes. (It's easier to handle the frozen decorations. They will defrost on the cake.)

## Short Pastry
(pie pastry)

2 cups all-purpose flour

¼ teaspoon salt

⅓ cup butter

⅓ cup shortening

6 tablespoons cold orange juice or
   ice water

**1** Sift flour and salt into bowl; add butter and shortening. Using pastry blender or fingers, blend together until mixture resembles coarse corn meal. Sprinkle with orange juice.

**2** Gather dough into a mass. Punch it down in bowl with fist and heel of hand 3 or 4 times.

**3** Shape dough into a ball. Cut in half; flatten each half slightly with heel of hand. Cover each half with plastic wrap and refrigerate at least 1 hour.

Makes enough for a 2-crust pie, 9 or 10 inches in diameter.

### Making a Pie Shell

All-purpose flour

½ recipe for Short Pastry (see preceding recipe)

**1** Place Short Pastry on floured board; sprinkle top with flour.

**2** With rolling pin, roll dough into a disc 13 inches in diameter and 1/16-inch thick.

**3** Fit pastry disc into 9-inch pie plate. To even edges, trim with scissors.

**4** Form a rim by turning under the overhanging dough to meet edge of pie plate. Crimp the rim.

**5** Prick pastry bottom with a fork. To make sure dough remains flat, press aluminum foil down on top of it. Fill with uncooked rice or beans.

**6** Bake in preheated 400-degree oven for 8 to 10 minutes. Remove foil and beans and continue baking pastry about 5 minutes more, until just lightly browned. Cool on wire rack.

# Apple Pie
# with Blossoms

This good old standard becomes something special when it's served up with flowers made of hard sauce.

   *Short Pastry (see recipe, page 118)*
 8 *large apples (McIntosh, Greenings or Cortlandts)*
¾ *cup granulated sugar*
 1 *teaspoon ground cinnamon*
 2 *tablespoons quick-cooking tapioca*
 1 *tablespoon butter*
   *Hard Sauce Blossoms (recipe follows)*

**1**   Roll out half of pie pastry and place in 9-inch pie plate. Prick surface with fork.

**2**   Pare and core apples; slice thinly. Place in bowl with sugar, cinnamon and tapioca. Mix thoroughly.

**3**   Pour into pastry-lined pie plate. Dot with butter.

**4**   Roll out other half of pastry dough and cover pie. Cut off uneven edges of dough; pinch top and bottom crusts together. Fold under to form a rim around outer edge of pie plate. Crimp.

**5**   Make several decorative slashes in top crust, and cut a small hole in the center.

**6**   Bake in preheated 400-degree oven for 50 minutes.

**7**   Just before serving, decorate top with Hard Sauce Blossoms. Serve warm or cold.

8 servings.

## Hard Sauce Blossoms

 ½ *cup butter, softened*
1½ *cups confectioners' sugar, sifted*
 2 *tablespoons rum*

**1**   Cream butter with sugar and rum.

**2**   Fill gun with mixture. Fit with star or flower disc.

**3**   Use gun at high speed. Press out flowers onto waxed paper-lined baking sheet, following directions for making pressed cookies (see page 9).

**4**   Refrigerate until hardened. Remove from waxed paper and place on fruit pie.

# Banana Cream Pie

Cream pie connoisseurs will go bananas over this. And who'd blame them?

*9-inch baked Pie Shell (see recipe, page 118)*

1 *envelope unflavored gelatin*

¼ *cup cold water*

6 *large egg yolks*

1 *cup granulated sugar*

1 *teaspoon banana or vanilla extract*

2½ *cups heavy cream*

4 *large ripe bananas*

2 *tablespoons apricot preserves*

1 *tablespoon confectioners' sugar, sifted*

**1**  Prepare Pie Shell as directed.

**2**  Sprinkle gelatin over cold water to soften. Stir over hot water to dissolve. Set aside to cool.

**3**  With mixer at medium to high speed, beat egg yolks until foamy. Gradually beat in sugar; continue beating until so thick that a ribbon forms on the surface when the beater is lifted. (This may take about 10 minutes).

**4**  Add banana or vanilla extract; stir. Add gelatin in a thin stream, beating constantly.

**5**  Whip 2 cups of heavy cream until stiff. Fold into mixture.

**6**  Slice about 2½ bananas into ⅛-inch rounds; cover bottom of baked Pie Shell with them. Mound the filling on top. Refrigerate until set.

**7**  Slice remaining bananas into ⅛-inch rounds. Make a ring of overlapping banana slices around rim of pie. Brush bananas with apricot preserves.

**8**  Whip remaining ½ cup of heavy cream with confectioners' sugar until stiff.

**9**  Fill gun with whipped cream. Fit with decorator tip.

**10**  Using gun at low speed, pipe cream onto center of pie in decorative design.

8 servings.

———

*Note:* Egg whites can be saved to make meringues or Crème Saint-Honoré. Store whites in freezer.

# Key
# Lime Pie

The tangy, cool and refreshing taste of lime is what makes this Florida meringue pie a favorite.

*9-inch baked Coconut Pie Pastry Shell (recipe follows)*
*4  large eggs, separated*
*⅓  cup lime juice*
*1¾  cups granulated sugar*
*5  tablespoons cornstarch*
*¼  teaspoon salt*
*1½  cups boiling water*
*1  tablespoon grated lime rind*
*2  tablespoons butter*
*Green food coloring*

**1**  Prepare Coconut Pie Pastry Shell as directed.

**2**  Combine egg yolks and lime juice; set aside.

**3**  In a heavy saucepan, combine 1¼ cups sugar, cornstarch and salt. Add boiling water, stirring constantly. Cook over medium heat; bring to a boil. Turn heat down to low; cook, stirring, for 2 more minutes.

**4**  Remove from heat; stir in the egg lime juice mixture. Return to heat; cook, stirring, for 2 more minutes until mixture thickens slightly.

**5**  Remove from heat. Stir in rind, butter and one or two drops of coloring until desired color is reached. Pour into Coconut Pie Pastry Shell.

**6**  Beat egg whites until soft peaks form. Gradually add remaining ½ cup sugar; beat until stiff and glossy.

**7**  Fill gun with meringue. Fit with decorator tip.

**8**  With gun at low speed, pipe mounds of meringue over surface of pie, making sure to touch crust.

**9**  Bake in preheated 350-degree oven for about 10 minutes until lightly browned. Refrigerate before serving.

6 to 8 servings.

**Coconut Pie Pastry Shell**

*⅓  cup butter, softened*
*3  tablespoons granulated sugar*
*1  large egg yolk*
*1  cup all-purpose flour, sifted*
*1  cup flaked coconut*

**1**  Cream butter and sugar. Add egg yolk; mix well. Add flour and mix. Stir in coconut.

**2**  Distribute mixture evenly along bottom and sides of 9-inch pie plate; press into place.

**3**  Bake in preheated 350-degree oven for 20 minutes.

**4**  Cool before filling.

# Chocolate Rum
# Chiffon Pie

*Chocolate Nut Pie Pastry Shell
(recipe follows)*

1  *envelope unflavored gelatin*

¼  *cup cold water*

2  *ounces unsweetened chocolate
squares*

1  *tablespoon strong black coffee*

⅔  *cup granulated sugar*

½  *cup hot milk*

2  *tablespoons rum*

1½  *cups heavy cream*

*Coffee Cream Topping
(recipe follows)*

**1**   Prepare Pastry Shell as directed.

**2**   Sprinkle gelatin over cold water to soften.

**3**   Melt chocolate over hot water. Add coffee, sugar and hot milk; cook for 3 minutes, stirring constantly.

**4**   Stir in gelatin; mix well. Remove from heat and place saucepan over ice water. Stir until cool and thickened. Add rum and mix well.

**5**   Beat 1½ cups heavy cream until stiff. Fold into chocolate mixture. Pile mixture into Chocolate Nut Pie Pastry Shell.

**6**   Fill gun with Coffee Cream Topping. Fit with decorator tip.

**7**   Using gun at low speed, pipe S-shaped squiggles around rim of pie. (The light coffee colored cream on the outside contrasts beautifully with the dark chocolate cream center.) Refrigerate.

8 servings.

## Chocolate Nut Pie Pastry Shell

1  *cup all-purpose flour*

⅓  *cup shortening*

3  *tablespoons ice water*

1  *ounce sweet baking chocolate, grated*

¼  *cup light brown sugar, packed*

¾  *cup finely chopped walnuts*

**1**   Place flour and shortening in a bowl. Using pastry blender or fingers, blend together until mixture is like coarse corn meal.

**2**   Sprinkle with ice water and gently combine, using fingers.

**3**   Add other ingredients; mix with a fork.

**4**   Press mixture firmly into a 9-inch pie plate, distributing it evenly.

**5**   Bake in preheated 375-degree oven for 15 minutes. Cool on wire rack.

Makes a 9-inch pie shell.

## Coffee Cream Topping

½  *cup heavy cream*

1  *teaspoon powdered instant coffee*

1½  *tablespoons confectioners' sugar, sifted*

Whip heavy cream with coffee and sugar until stiff. Makes 1 cup.

# Toasted Coconut
# Cream Pie

*9-inch baked Graham Cracker Crust
(recipe follows)*

1½  *cups flaked coconut*

⅓  *cup all-purpose flour*

¾  *cup granulated sugar*

2  *cups light cream*

¼  *teaspoon salt*

4  *large eggs, separated*

2  *teaspoons vanilla extract*

**1**   Prepare Graham Cracker Crust as directed.

**2**   Place coconut on baking pan in preheated 350-degree oven for 10 to 15 minutes until it turns light brown. Check it often and stir. Set aside to cool.

**3**   Combine flour, ¼ cup sugar, cream and salt. Cook over boiling water, stirring, until sauce is smooth and thick.

**4**   Stir a little of the hot sauce into egg yolks. Add this mixture to balance of hot sauce in pot; stir. Add 1 cup of the coconut. Cook over hot water, stirring, for another 3 minutes. Remove from heat; add vanilla and stir.

**5**   Pour coconut cream mixture into baked Graham Cracker Crust.

**6**   Beat 4 egg whites with remaining ½ cup of sugar until stiff and glossy.

**7**   Fill gun with meringue. Fit with decorator tip.

**8**   Using gun at high speed, pipe meringue mounds over the entire surface of pie, making sure to touch edges of crust.

**9**   Bake in preheated 350-degree oven for about 15 minutes until lightly browned.

**10**   Refrigerate. Before serving, sprinkle pie with balance of coconut.

8 servings.

## Graham Cracker Crust

1¼  *cups graham cracker crumbs*

¼  *cup granulated sugar*

¼  *cup butter, softened*

**1**   Mix ingredients together in a bowl. Press mixture into 9-inch pie plate firmly and evenly.

**2**   Bake in preheated 375-degree oven for 8 minutes. Cool on wire rack.

## Pecan Pie

Rich and delicious! An American favorite.

½   recipe Short Pastry (see page 118)
2½  tablespoons granulated sugar
4   tablespoons flour
2   cups light corn syrup
5   large eggs, well beaten
¾   teaspoon salt
1¼  teaspoons vanilla extract
3   tablespoons melted butter
    Pecan halves
½   cup heavy cream
1½  tablespoons confectioners' sugar,
    sifted

1   Prepare Short Pastry as directed. Roll out dough; place in 9-inch pie plate. Prick bottom surface with fork. Set aside.

2   Place sugar, flour and corn syrup in a bowl; mix well. Beat in eggs, salt and vanilla. Add butter; mix thoroughly.

3   Pour into reserved pastry shell. Cover filling with pecans.

4   Bake in preheated 350-degree oven for about 50 minutes, until a sharp knife inserted in custard comes out clean. Cool on wire rack.

5   Whip heavy cream with confectioners' sugar until stiff.

6   Fill gun with whipped cream. Fit with decorator tip.

7   Using gun at low speed, pipe decorative border around rim of pie.

Serves 6 to 8.

## Angels' Nest with Strawberries

Simple to make—and heavenly.

1½  cups heavy cream
¼   cup confectioners' sugar, sifted
2   teaspoons vanilla extract
2   pints fresh strawberries, hulled
    Additional confectioners' sugar,
    sifted

1   Whip heavy cream with sugar and vanilla until very stiff.

2   Using some of the additional sugar, outline an 8- to 9-inch circle on a crystal cake stand.

3   Fill gun with whipped cream. Fit with decorator tip.

4   Using gun at high speed, pipe cream around the circle, forming a nest. (Let cream fall almost at random, piling up in zig-zag fashion.)

5   Place strawberries inside the nest. Sprinkle berries with remaining sugar.

6 to 8 servings.

## Buttercream Cake

This cake freezes well with its filling.

½ cup butter, softened

1 cup granulated sugar

2 large eggs, separated

2 teaspoons vanilla extract

1½ cups cake flour

1½ teaspoons baking powder

½ cup milk

Coffee Buttercream Filling (recipe follows)

Confectioners' sugar, sifted

**1** With mixer at medium to high speed, cream butter with sugar until very light and fluffy. Add egg yolks one at a time, beating well after each addition. Beat in vanilla.

**2** Sift together flour and baking powder. Alternately add flour and milk to butter mixture, beginning and ending with flour. Beat well after each addition.

**3** Beat egg whites until stiff; fold into batter.

**4** Grease and flour a 10 x 6-inch baking pan. Pour in batter. Bake in preheated 350-degree oven for 20 to 25 minutes, until cake tester comes out clean. Cool on wire rack for 10 minutes; turn out of pan.

**5** When completely cool, level cake top and split cake in half horizontally.

**6** Fill gun with Coffee Buttercream. Fit with decorator tip.

**7** Using gun at high speed, pipe mounds of buttercream on bottom layer of cake.

Mounds should be ¾-inch high with ¼-inch spaces between them. (For decorative purposes, pipe cream as close to cake rim as possible.) Cover gently with top layer of cake. Sprinkle heavily with confectioners' sugar. Refrigerate.

12 servings.

### Coffee Buttercream Filling

5 large egg yolks

½ cup cold strong coffee

¼ cup granulated sugar

1 teaspoon unsweetened dark cocoa

1 cup butter, softened

½ cup heavy cream

**1** Combine egg yolks, coffee and sugar in a saucepan. Cook over low heat, stirring constantly with a wooden spoon, until mixture thinly coats the spoon. Do not let it boil.

**2** Place saucepan in a bowl of ice water; stir until mixture is barely warm.

**3** Transfer mixture to a bowl. Add cocoa. With mixer at high speed, beat until thick enough for ribbon to form on surface when mixture falls from beater. Beat in butter, a little at a time, until thoroughly mixed.

**4** Whip heavy cream until stiff; fold into mixture. Refrigerate for 1 hour.

————

Note: Egg whites may be saved for meringues or Crème Saint-Honoré. Store whites in freezer.

# Christmas Cassata

This cake is a blend of unusual flavors. It is elegant yet simple to make.

*Pound cake loaf (about 8 inches long)*
*15-ounce container ricotta cheese*
*¼ cup granulated sugar*
*3 tablespoons orange flavored liqueur (Triple Sec or Cointreau)*
*3 tablespoons diced candied fruits (fruit cake mix)*
*2 ounces semi-sweet chocolate squares, coarsely chopped*
*Chocolate Frosting (recipe follows)*
*3 Icing Cream Decorations in the form of green Christmas trees (see recipe, page 117)*

**1** Cut off crusts of pound cake; level the top. Slice cake horizontally into 3 equal layers.

**2** With beater on medium to high speed, beat ricotta with sugar and liqueur until smooth. Fold in fruits and chocolate, using rubber spatula.

**3** Spread half the cheese mixture over bottom layer of cake; top with middle layer; spread with remaining cheese mixture. Place last layer on top. Gently press the loaf together, making it as compact as possible. Refrigerate for 2 to 3 hours.

**4** Using a spatula, completely cover cake with Chocolate Frosting. Reserve some frosting in refrigerator until quite firm but not hard.

**5** Fill gun with firm frosting. Fit with decorator tip.

**6** Using gun at high speed, pipe a decorative border around bottom and top of cake.

**7** Arrange 3 Icing Cream Decorations (Christmas trees) on top of cake.

12 servings.

## Chocolate Frosting

*6 ounces semi-sweet chocolate squares*
*¼ cup strong black coffee*
*¾ cup confectioners' sugar, sifted*
*½ cup butter*
*⅓ cup sour cream*

**1** Melt chocolate with coffee over hot water. Add sugar; mix well. Remove from heat.

**2** Add butter in pieces, mixing well after each addition until smooth. Add sour cream; mix well. Refrigerate until thick enough to spread.

# Tipsy Parson

The traditional English "trifle." So sinfully good!

½ loaf of pound cake
3 tablespoons cooking sherry
⅓ cup apricot preserves
5 almond macaroons
1½ tablespoons cognac
   Crème Anglaise (recipe follows)
   Meringue Topping (recipe follows)

**1**   Cover bottom of a 1½-quart glass soufflé dish with a layer of pound cake ¾-inch thick. Sprinkle with sherry; spread on a layer of apricot preserves; crumble macaroons on top; sprinkle with cognac; cover with warm Crème Anglaise. Refrigerate.

**2**   Prepare Meringue Topping (using 4 egg whites instead of the usual 3).

**3**   Fill gun with Meringue Topping. Fit with decorator tip.

**4**   Using gun at low speed, pipe 2-inch high peaks on top of Crème, starting from the edges of the dish and working towards center. (This prevents meringue from shrinking.)

**5**   Bake in preheated 425-degree oven for 4 to 6 minutes.

8 servings.

## Crème Anglaise (custard cream)

4 large egg yolks (reserve whites for Meringue Topping)
6 tablespoons granulated sugar
1 cup heavy cream
1 cup milk
1 teaspoon vanilla extract
1 tablespoon cognac

**1**   In heavy saucepan, combine egg yolks with sugar; mix thoroughly with a wire whisk.

**2**   Very slowly pour cream and milk into egg sugar mixture, stirring constantly. Cook over medium low heat, stirring constantly with a wooden spoon, until custard thinly coats the spoon.

**3**   Remove from heat; stir for another minute. Add vanilla and cognac; stir well. Cool at room temperature for half an hour. Refrigerate.

Makes about 2½ cups of custard sauce.

## Meringue Topping

3 egg whites (for Tipsy Parson, use 4 egg whites)
6 tablespoons granulated sugar

Beat egg whites until light and foamy or until soft peaks form. Gradually add sugar, beating continually until meringue is stiff and glossy.

# Paris-Brest
# with Cream

A most elegant dessert. Delicate pastry and whipped vanilla cream.

Pâte à Choux (see recipe, page 57)

1  egg

2  tablespoons milk

¼  cup sliced almonds

2½  cups heavy cream

½  cup confectioners' sugar, sifted

2½  teaspoons vanilla extract

Additional confectioners' sugar, sifted

1  Prepare Pâte à Choux as directed, through step 2.

2  Trace an 8-inch diameter circle on a greased and floured baking sheet.

3  Fill gun with Pâte à Choux. Fit with decorator tip.

4  Use gun at high speed. Pipe mixture into a circle of attached mounds, using the tracing as a guide. The mounds should be about 1½ inches wide and 1½ inches high.

5  Combine egg and milk; beat lightly. Brush ring with egg mixture; sprinkle almonds on top.

6  Bake in preheated 450-degree oven for 15 minutes. Reduce temperature to 350 degrees; bake about 35 minutes more, until sides are dry and rigid and ring is nicely browned.

7  Make a few slits on the side of the ring with a small sharp knife. Remove from pan and cool on wire rack.

8  Whip heavy cream with confectioners' sugar and vanilla until stiff.

9  Carefully split pastry ring horizontally. Fill bottom layer with whipped cream, reserving some for decoration. Replace top of pastry.

10  Fill gun with remaining whipped cream. Fit with decorator tip.

11  Using gun at high speed, pipe 5 or 6 rosettes around top of ring.

12  Sift additional confectioners' sugar on top. Refrigerate.

8 servings.

# Cookies and Candies

In many homes cookie-baking has become an art lost in the misty traditions of yester-year, when time seemed to be less pressing. Now, fortunately, the tide is turning. More and more people are rediscovering the simple joys of home baking, with those rich, heady aromas we cherished as children once more drifting through the house. The cookie jar is a symbol of a loving, ordered home; keeping it well-stocked is no problem with the foodgun. You can turn out large batches with ease, each batch perfectly uniform. Candies, too, will have that "professional" look.

If you store cookies in tightly covered containers, they should stay fresh for weeks. Candies keep best when refrigerated.

## Molasses and Spice

Brown sugar and spice and everything nice . . . that's what these cookies are made of.

¼  *cup butter, softened*
¼  *cup shortening*
¼  *cup granulated sugar*
¼  *cup dark brown sugar, packed*
 1  *large egg*
 2  *tablespoons molasses*
1½  *cups all-purpose flour*
 ½  *teaspoon ground cinnamon*
 ½  *teaspoon ground ginger*
 ½  *teaspoon ground cloves*
 ½  *teaspoon ground nutmeg*
 ⅛  *teaspoon salt*

**1**   With mixer at medium to high speed, cream butter and shortening with both sugars until fluffy. Add egg and molasses; beat thoroughly.

**2**   Sift flour with spices and salt. Add to molasses mixture in several additions, beating well after each addition.

**3**   Cover dough completely with plastic wrap. Refrigerate for half an hour.

**4**   Fill gun with dough. Fit with desired cookie disc.

**5**   Use gun at high speed. Follow instructions for making pressed cookies (see page 9). Use ungreased cookie sheets.

**6**   Bake in preheated 375-degree oven for 8 to 10 minutes. Be careful not to burn cookies. Remove from cookie sheets and cool on wire rack.

Makes about 6 dozen cookies.

## Sweet Hearts and Flowers

Delectable Danish butter cookies with an almond flavor.

¾  *cup butter*
 1  *large egg*
 ½  *cup granulated sugar*
 ½  *teaspoon almond extract*
 ⅛  *cup blanched almonds*
2⅛  *cups all-purpose flour*
    *Confectioners' sugar, sifted*

**1**   Melt butter over low heat. Set aside to cool.

**2**   With mixer at medium to high speed, beat egg, sugar and almond extract until thoroughly combined.

**3**   Grate almonds until fine in blender or Mouli grater. Place in strainer and sift into egg sugar mixture; stir. (Do not use nuts that won't fit through strainer.)

**4**   Add flour in several additions, beating well after each addition. Add cooled butter; mix well.

**5**   Cover dough completely with plastic wrap and refrigerate for about ½ hour.

**6**   Fill gun with dough. Fit alternately with heart and flower discs.

**7**   Use gun at high speed. Follow instructions for making pressed cookies (see page 9). Use ungreased cookie sheets.

**8**   Bake for about 10 minutes in preheated 375-degree oven until cookies just start to turn light golden around edges. Remove from cookie sheets and roll in confectioners' sugar while still warm. Cool on wire rack.

Makes 5 to 6 dozen cookies.

## Chocolate Cake Cookies

These cookies have an interesting cake-like texture.

1½   ounces semi-sweet chocolate squares
1⅔   cups all-purpose flour
 ¾   cup granulated sugar
 ½   teaspoon salt
 ½   teaspoon baking soda
 ½   cup butter
 ½   teaspoon vanilla extract
  1   large egg, beaten
 ½   cup sour cream
     Additional granulated sugar

**1**  Melt chocolate over hot water. Cool at room temperature.

**2**  Sift next four ingredients into bowl. Add butter; blend together, using fingers or pastry blender.

**3**  Mix vanilla, egg and sour cream together. Add to butter mixture; blend thoroughly with wooden spoon.

**4**  Add melted chocolate; mix thoroughly.

**5**  Cover bowl with plastic wrap and refrigerate for 1½ hours.

**6**  Fill gun with dough. Fit alternately with star, diamond and saw-toothed discs. (When using saw-toothed disc, cut cookies after baking.)

**7**  Use gun at high speed. Follow instructions for making pressed cookies (see page 9). Use ungreased cookie sheets.

**8**  Bake in preheated 400-degree oven for about 10 minutes. Remove from cookie sheets and roll in additional sugar while still warm. Cool on wire rack.

Makes 3 to 4 dozen cookies.

*Shown right, Surprise de Boule Etoilée (p. 107).*

# Danish
# Cookie Wreaths

The colors are marvelously appropriate for the Christmas season . . . but the cookies taste just as delicious any other time of year.

 2   cups plus 2 tablespoons all-purpose flour
1¼  cups granulated sugar
 1   cup plus 2 tablespoons butter, softened
 1   teaspoon vanilla extract
 1   large egg yolk
 ⅔   cup blanched almonds
     Red and green candied cherries (optional)

**1**   Sift flour and sugar together into a bowl. Add butter and vanilla; blend together with fingers or pastry blender until mixture is like coarse corn meal. Add egg yolk and mix well.

**2**   Grate almonds until fine in blender or Mouli grater. Place in strainer and sift into butter mixture. (Do not use nuts that won't fit through strainer.) Stir with fork until well mixed.

**3**   Fill gun with dough. Fit with decorator tip.

**4**   Use gun at high speed. On ungreased cookie sheets, press out 5 or 6 rows of dough, each as long as the cookie sheet. Cut rows into 3-inch strips; shape each strip into a wreath, pressing the ends together gently. Arrange wreaths 1 inch apart on cookie sheets.

**5**   Cut red and green candied cherries into small pieces; press them into wreaths to decorate (optional). Refrigerate for 30 minutes before baking.

**6**   Bake in preheated 375-degree oven for 8 minutes until cookies just turn golden. Remove from cookie sheets and cool on wire rack.

Makes about 10 dozen cookies.

Shown left, Christmas Cassata (p. 126), Pistachio Cream Meringue (p. 109), Coconut Orange Glace (p. 112).

## Citrus Cookie Sandwiches

Tangy tidbits with a marmalade middle.

¾   cup butter, softened
½   cup granulated sugar
 1   large egg
 2   tablespoons orange juice
2¼   cups all-purpose flour
 ½   teaspoon baking powder
 ¼   teaspoon salt
     Orange, grapefruit or lemon
         marmalade

**1**   With mixer at medium to high speed, cream butter with sugar until light and fluffy. Add egg and juice; beat well.

**2**   Sift together flour, baking powder and salt. Add to butter sugar mixture in several additions, beating well after each addition.

**3**   Completely cover dough with plastic wrap and refrigerate for 1 hour.

**4**   Fill gun with dough. Fit with any cookie disc except saw-toothed or dog disc.

**5**   Use gun at high speed. Follow instructions for making pressed cookies (see page 9). Use ungreased cookie sheets.

**6**   Bake in preheated 375-degree oven for about 10 minutes until cookies are firm but not brown. Remove from cookie sheets and cool on wire racks.

**7**   When completely cool, make cookie sandwiches, putting marmalade in the middle.

Makes 2 to 3 dozen sandwiches.

## Pressed Lemon Zests

Pressed cookies that look and taste good enough to please all lemon lovers.

 1   cup butter, softened
     3-ounce package cream cheese
 1   cup granulated sugar
 1   large egg
 1   tablespoon lemon juice
 2   teaspoons grated lemon rind
 6   drops yellow food coloring
2¾   cups all-purpose flour
 ½   teaspoon baking powder

**1**   With mixer at medium to high speed, cream butter and cheese together. Add sugar; beat until light and fluffy.

**2**   Add egg, lemon juice, lemon rind and coloring; beat well.

**3**   Sift together flour and baking powder. Add to cheese mixture in several additions, beating well after each addition.

**4**   Completely cover dough in plastic wrap and refrigerate for 1 hour.

**5**   Fill gun with dough. Fit with diamond, star or flower discs.

**6**   Use gun at low speed. Follow instructions for making pressed cookies (see page 9). Use ungreased cookie sheets.

**7**   Bake in preheated 375-degree oven for about 10 minutes, until cookies just start to turn light golden around edges. Remove from sheets and cool on wire rack.

Makes about 8 dozen cookies.

## Shortbread Stars and Stripes

1   cup butter, softened
½   cup confectioners' sugar, sifted
1   teaspoon vanilla extract
2   cups all-purpose flour
¼   teaspoon baking powder
    Tiny silver ball candy decorations
    Red decorating sugar

**1**   With mixer at medium to high speed, cream butter with sugar and vanilla until light and fluffy.

**2**   Sift together flour and baking powder. Add to butter sugar mixture in several additions, beating after each addition.

**3**   Completely cover dough in plastic wrap and refrigerate for ½ hour.

**4**   Fill gun with dough. Fit with saw-toothed disc to get stripe effect. (Any of the discs may be used to make cookies with this shortbread recipe.)

**5**   Use gun at high speed. Follow instructions for making cookie fingers (see page 9). Use ungreased baking sheets. If the dough ripples as it's squeezed out, that's fine. The cookies will look more like flags.

**6**   Cut dough into 2½-inch strips; decorate like flags. For "stars," press silver balls into upper left corner of cookies; for "stripes," sprinkle 2 or 3 rows of red sugar along cookie ridges.

**7**   Bake in preheated 375-degree oven for about 7 minutes, until cookies just start to turn light golden around edges. Remove from sheets and cool on wire rack.

Makes 4 to 5 dozen flags.

## Meringue Kisses

These delicate confections will stand up in perky peaks.

4   large egg whites, at room temperature
1   cup granulated sugar
1   teaspoon vanilla extract
    Chocolate mini-bits

**1**   Beat egg whites until foamy. Add sugar and vanilla a spoonful at a time, beating continuously, until meringue is smooth, glossy and stiff.

**2**   Line cookie sheets with waxed paper.

**3**   Fill gun with meringue. Fit with decorator tip.

**4**   Using gun at low speed, form small mounds on cookie sheet 1 inch apart.

**5**   Sprinkle chocolate bits over some of the mounds and leave some plain.

**6**   Bake in preheated 250-degree oven for about 50 minutes until cookies turn a pale beige color. Remove from waxed paper; cool on wire rack. If meringue sticks to paper, place paper on damp cloth for a minute.

Makes about 4 dozen meringue kisses.

___

*Note:* Yolks may be saved to make egg custard. Store unbroken yolks in a jar with water to cover; refrigerate.

## Chocolate Peanut Butter Sticks

These little sticks have a flavor all their own. Sure to be snapped up.

¼  cup butter, softened
¼  cup shortening
½  cup peanut butter
½  cup granulated sugar
½  cup dark brown sugar, packed
1  large egg
1¼  cups all-purpose flour
½  teaspoon baking powder
½  teaspoon baking soda
¼  teaspoon salt
5  ounces semi-sweet chocolate squares
1  cup finely chopped salted peanuts

**1**  With mixer at medium to high speed, cream butter, shortening, peanut butter and both sugars. Add egg; beat thoroughly.

**2**  Sift together flour, baking powder, baking soda and salt. Add to peanut butter mixture in several additions, beating well after each addition.

**3**  Completely cover dough in plastic wrap and refrigerate for ½ hour.

**4**  Fill gun with dough. Fit with decorator tip.

**5**  Use gun at high speed. On lightly greased cookie sheets, press out 5 or 6 rows of dough, evenly spaced, each as long as the cookie sheet.

**6**  Bake in preheated 375-degree oven for 8 to 10 minutes, until very lightly browned. Do not overbake. Cut into 2½-inch sticks. Remove from cookie sheets and cool on wire rack.

**7**  Melt chocolate over hot water. Remove from heat.

**8**  When cookies are cool, dip one end of the ridged side into melted chocolate, then into nuts.

Makes 8 to 9 dozen cookies.

## Frosted Orange Cookies

The flaky texture of the cookie plus the tangy sweetness of the icing make these drop cookies a special favorite with children.

⅓  cup butter, softened

⅓  cup shortening

¾  cup granulated sugar

 1  large egg

 2  cups all-purpose flour

½  teaspoon baking powder

½  teaspoon baking soda

½  teaspoon salt

 2  tablespoons grated orange rind

½  cup orange juice

    Orange Icing (recipe follows)

**1**  With mixer at medium to high speed, cream butter and shortening with sugar until light and fluffy. Add egg and beat thoroughly.

**2**  Sift together flour, baking powder, baking soda and salt.

**3**  In separate bowl, combine grated rind and orange juice. Alternately add juice and flour to butter mixture in several additions, beating well after each addition.

**4**  Fill gun with dough. Fit with decorator tip.

**5**  Using gun at low speed, form small mounds on ungreased cookie sheet 1 inch apart.

**6**  Bake in preheated 400-degree oven for 8 to 10 minutes, until just starting to turn golden around edges. Remove from cookie sheets and cool on wire racks.

**7**  Spread Orange Icing on tops of cookies using circular motion. (It's easiest to do this with your finger.)

Makes 5 to 6 dozen cookies.

### Orange Icing

1½  tablespoons butter, softened

 1  cup confectioners' sugar, sifted

 1  tablespoon orange juice

 1  tablespoon grated orange rind

 1  drop red food coloring

 2  drops yellow food coloring

Beat butter and sugar. Add other ingredients; blend until smooth.

# Chocolate Banana Shells

These delicious cookies actually look like beautiful sea shells. (Put one to your ear and you'll hear distant calls of "More! More!")

6-ounce package *semi-sweet chocolate pieces*
⅓  *cup butter, softened*
⅓  *cup shortening*
1  *cup granulated sugar*
2  *large eggs*
1  *teaspoon vanilla extract*
2¼  *cups all-purpose flour*
2  *teaspoons baking powder*
½  *teaspoon salt*
1  *cup mashed ripe bananas*
*Additional granulated sugar*

**1**  Melt chocolate over hot water. Cool at room temperature.

**2**  With mixer at medium to high speed, cream butter, shortening and sugar until light and fluffy. Add eggs and vanilla; beat thoroughly.

**3**  Add melted chocolate to butter mixture; stir thoroughly.

**4**  Sift together flour, baking powder and salt. Add alternately with bananas to chocolate batter, beating well after each addition.

**5**  Fill gun with batter. Fit with decorator tip.

**6**  Using gun at low speed, form small mounds 1½ inches apart on ungreased cookie sheets.

**7**  Bake in preheated 375-degree oven for 10 or 12 minutes until set. Remove from cookie sheets; roll in additional granulated sugar while still warm. Cool on wire rack.

Makes about 7 dozen cookies.

## Coconut Almond Crunchies

A macaroon-like cookie, crunchy on the outside and soft inside.

1½   cups blanched almonds
 3   large egg whites, at room temperature
1¼   cups granulated sugar
 ¼   teaspoon salt
 1   teaspoon almond extract
 1   cup flaked coconut
     Candied cherries and/or blanched
       almonds

**1**   Grate nuts until fine in electric blender or Mouli grater. Set aside.

**2**   With mixer at high speed, beat egg whites until foamy. Beat in sugar and salt, adding a little at a time. Continue beating until very stiff and glossy.

**3**   Using a wooden spoon, stir in almond extract. Place grated nuts in strainer and sift into sugar and egg mixture. (Do not use nuts that won't fit through strainer.) Add coconut; mix well.

**4**   Fill gun with mixture. Fit with decorator tip.

**5**   Using gun at high speed, press out small mounds, 2 inches apart, on cookie sheets lined with ungreased brown paper (from grocery bags, etc.). Place a piece of candied cherry or a blanched almond in center of each mound.

**6**   Bake in preheated 325-degree oven for about 15 minutes, until set and delicately brown. Do not overbake.

**7**   Remove paper with baked cookies from cookie sheet. Lay wet towel on hot cookie sheet; put paper with cookies on top of towel. Leave for 1 minute until steam loosens cookies. Remove with spatula; cool on wire rack.

Makes 3 to 4 dozen cookies.

## Dark Chocolates

Once you try these, you may never want store-bought chocolates again.

4 4-ounce packages sweet chocolate
2 eggs
¼ cup butter, softened
  Maraschino cherries
  Pecan halves
  Almonds

**1**  Melt chocolate over hot water. Remove from heat. Add eggs; stir until smooth. Mix in butter. Cool for about 15 minutes.

**2**  Cut cherries in half and pat dry. Arrange them about 1½ to 2 inches apart, cut side down, in baking pans lined with oiled waxed paper. Also lay out pecans and almonds in the lined baking pans.

**3**  Fill gun with chocolate mixture. Fit with decorator tip.

**4**  Using gun at low speed, pipe chocolate over the cherries and nuts, forming individual candies. Refrigerate to harden.

Makes about 5 dozen candies.

————

Variation: Date pieces and flaked coconut may be used along with or instead of nuts and cherries. Plain chocolate candies may also be made.

## Fudge Fantasy

Delicious old-fashioned chocolaty fudge crafted into individual flower and animal shapes.

4 ounces unsweetened chocolate
    squares
½ cup butter
1 large egg
1 pound confectioners' sugar
¼ cup sweetened condensed milk
1 teaspoon vanilla extract

**1**  Melt chocolate with butter over hot water.

**2**  In a bowl, beat egg lightly. Mix with sugar. Add chocolate mixture, milk and vanilla; mix well. Cover and refrigerate for 15 minutes.

**3**  Fill gun with mixture. Fit with desired disc.

**4**  Using gun at high speed, press out fudge forms onto greased baking pan. Follow instructions for making pressed cookies and fudge (see page 9). Refrigerate to harden.

Makes about 6 dozen candies.

## Marzipan
## Posies

A gay platter of marzipan flowers adds a festive touch.

    *8-ounce can almond paste*
¼   *cup softened butter*
2   *tablespoons light corn syrup*
1¼  *cups confectioners' sugar, sifted*
    *Assorted food colorings*

**1**   Using wooden spoon, blend almond paste and butter in bowl. Add corn syrup and sugar; mix together with spoon. (If dough comes out too soft, add more confectioners' sugar.)

**2**   Divide mixture into quarters and color each differently by adding drops of food color.

**3**   Fill gun with one color of the mixture at a time. Fit with desired disc.

**4**   Use gun at high speed. Press out shapes onto ungreased cookie sheet, following instructions for making pressed cookies and fudge (see page 9).

**5**   Place sheet of candies in refrigerator to harden. Remove with a spatula.

Makes about 5 dozen candies.

# Index

# PARTY LOG

| Date / Event | Guests | Menu |
| --- | --- | --- |
| | | |
| | | |
| | | |
| | | |
| | | |
| | | |
| | | |